JUDAISM
WORLD RELIGIONS
REVISED EDITION

by
Martha A. Morrison
Stephen F. Brown

☑® Facts On File, Inc.

JUDAISM, Revised Edition
World Religions

Copyright © 2002, 1991 by Martha A. Morrison and Stephen F. Brown

Facts On File, Inc.
132 West 31st Street
New York NY 10001

Library of Congress Cataloging-in-Publication Data
Morrison, M. A. (Martha A.)
Judaism / by Martha Morrison, Stephen F. Brown.—Rev. ed.
    p. cm. — (World religions)
Summary: An account of the history and rituals of Judaism, examining such areas as sacred use of the Hebrew language and the role of the faith in establishing the contemporary nation of Israel.
Includes bibliographical references and index.
    ISBN 0-8160-4766-9
    1. Judaism [1.Judaism.] I. Brown, Stephen F. II. Title. III. Series.
BM561.M67 2002
296—dc21   200202363

Developed by Brown Publishing Network, Inc. Series design by Trelawney Goodell. Design Production by Jennifer J. Angell/ Brown Publishing Network, Inc. Photo Research by Picture Vision, Nina Whitney and Libby Taft.

Photo credits:
Cover: David Bartruff/©CORBIS; *Title page:* A boy holding the Torah during the celebration of his bar mitzvah. Ted Spiegel/©CORBIS; *Table of Contents page:* A devout Jew praying at Jerusalem's Western or Wailing Wall. Charles Lenars/©CORBIS; *Pages 6–7:* Lawrence Migdale/Getty Images; *13:* Roger Ressmeyer/©CORBIS; *18–19:* Chase Swift/©CORBIS; *25:* North Wind Picture Archives; *28:* Marburg/Art Resource, New York; *33:* North Wind Picture Archives; *40:* Robert Holmes/©CORBIS; *46–47:* Clemens Kalischer/Image Photos; *50:* David Bartruff/©CORBIS; *59:* Clemens Kalischer/Image Photos; *65:* Byron Rollins/AP Wide World Photos; *67:* David Rubinger/©CORBIS; *70-71:* Paul A. Souders/©CORBIS; *74:* PictureQuest; *79:* North Wind Picture Archives; *84:* Bettman/©CORBIS; *86–87:* Bettman/©CORBIS; *96:* Clemens Kalischer/Image Photos; *98:* Seth Joel/©CORBIS; *100:* Coutesy of Touro Synagogue. Photo: John I. Hopf; *104–105:* Clemens Kalischer/Image Photos; *109:* Clemens Kalischer/Image Photos; *112:* Clemens Kalischer/Image Photos; *116–117:* Farrell Grehan/©CORBIS; *120:* Bettman/©CORBIS; *125:* AP Wide World Photos; *126:* Richard T. Nowitz©CORBIS; *130:* Clemens Kalischer/Image Photos; *132–133:* Clemens Kalischer/Image Photos; *137:* Reuters NewMedia Inc./©CORBIS.

Printed in the United States of America

VB PKG 10 9 8 7 6 5 4 3 2 1

This book is printed on acid-free paper.

TABLE OF CONTENTS

Preface   4

CHAPTER 1   Introduction: The Modern Jewish World   6

CHAPTER 2   Early History of the Jews and Judaism   18

CHAPTER 3   The Restoration to the Present   46

CHAPTER 4   The Hebrew Bible: An Overview   70

CHAPTER 5   Branches of Judaism and Their Basic Beliefs   86

CHAPTER 6   Rites of Passage   104

CHAPTER 7   The Impact of Judaism   116

CHAPTER 8   Judaism Facing the Future   132

Glossary   140

For Further Reading   142

Index   143

Preface

We live in what is sometimes described as a "secular age," meaning, in effect, that religion is not an especially important issue for most people. But there is much evidence to suggest that this is not true. In many societies, including the United States, religion and religious values shape the lives of millions of individuals and play a key role in politics and culture as well.

The World Religions series, of which this book is a part, is designed to appeal to both students and general readers. The books offer clear, accessible overviews of the major religious traditions and institutions of our time. Each volume in the series describes where a particular religion is practiced, its origins and history, its central beliefs and important rituals, and its contributions to world civilization. Carefully chosen photographs complement the text, and a glossary and bibliography are included to help readers gain a more complete understanding of the subject at hand.

Religious institutions and spirituality have always played a central role in world history. These books will help clarify what religion is all about and reveal both the similarities and differences in the great spiritual traditions practiced around the world today.

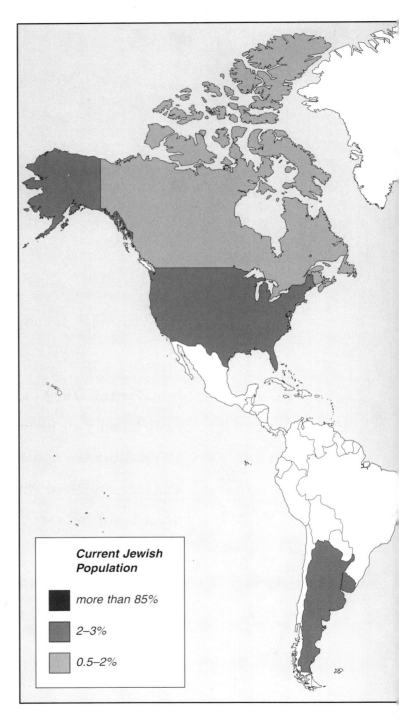

Current Jewish Population

more than 85%

2–3%

0.5–2%

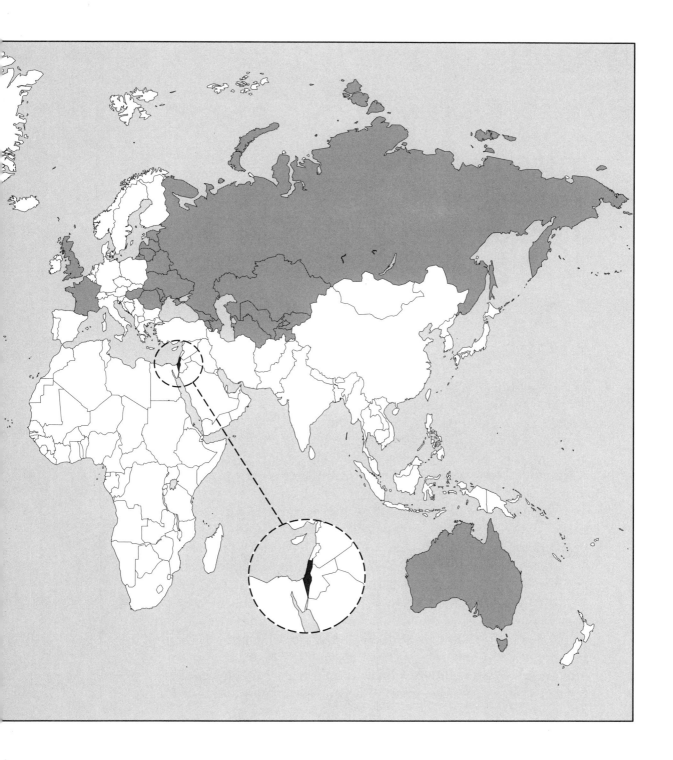

CHAPTER 1

Introduction:
The Modern
Jewish World

*J*udaism, whose followers are known as the Jews, is one of the world's most long-lived religious traditions. This respected ancient religion arose in the Near East some 3,500 years ago, in the mid-second millennium B.C.E. (before the common era), or 1500 B.C. Among monotheistic religions, or those whose followers believe in only one true god, it is most probably the oldest.

Though this religion has always had a relatively small number of believers, Judaism has played an extremely important role in the development of Western and Near Eastern civilizations. Christianity was built on the foundation of Judaism, and Islam, another great monotheistic tradition, was influenced by Judaism. Moreover, the Jews have risen to great heights in every area of cultural achievement. It is important to know that the Jews have made their contributions in the face of enormous difficulties, for their history has been a struggle for survival in an often hostile world. Only a tenacious adherence to their beliefs, their customs, and their identity accounts for their continued existence.

Terms

■ *Preceding page-Children, preparing for bar mitzvah and bat mitzvah, study the Torah in the synagogue.*

There are several terms related to the followers of Judaism that are often used in the same way yet have different meanings. The words *Hebrew, Israelite, Jew,* and even *Israeli* describe groups of people from different times in the history of Judaism.

The Hebrews were members of the various tribes who accepted Yahweh (Jehovah, in English form) as their one god. The term *Hebrew* is usually used to describe the Jews who lived from the earliest times to the end of the second millennium B.C.E. At that time, the Hebrews conquered the land of Canaan and settled there. In Genesis 10, a book of the Hebrew Bible, Eber is said to be an ancestor of the Hebrews. There is, however, evidence that the name *Eber* and the term *Hebrew* are not related. Other Near Eastern sources refer to people called *Apiru* or *Habiru,* most likely the root of the word *Hebrew.* These words are thought to have meant "outsider" or "wanderer."

The term *Israelite* describes two groups of people. In general, the Israelites were the descendants of the Hebrews, probably joined by other peoples, who created the united nation of ancient Israel around 1025 B.C.E. The word is also used to describe the people who inhabited the Northern Kingdom of Israel from about 922 to 722 B.C.E. Because all the peoples who inhabited Israel were related to the Hebrews and to each other, they all are considered to have been an ethnic group. Because the tribes of the Northern Kingdom of Israel formed a nation, they are considered a national group.

The word *Jew* comes from the term *yehudah,* or Judah. Judah, the Southern Kingdom of Israel that existed from about 922 to 586 B.C.E., was named after one of the many tribes that formed the people of Israel. Eventually Judah became more formally a religious state, dedicating its people to live as God's loyal followers. In Latin, the name of this Southern Kingdom was Judaea, and the term *Jew* comes from the Latin *Judaeus,* meaning "a resident of Judaea." After 70 C.E. (common era), or 70 A.D., the people of Judaea were scattered throughout the world. They retained the name *Judaeus,* which became shortened to *Jew.* Their religious and cultural practices became known as the Jewish way of life.

Today, the term *Jew* is used more broadly to refer to a member of a religious or cultural group, not an ethnic or national group. Someone who practices the religion of Judaism is a Jew. Someone who comes from a Jewish background and shares in Jewish culture is also a Jew. According to traditional Jewish law, a Jew is either a person whose mother is Jewish or who has converted to the faith under the supervision of a rabbi.

Jews are found in many countries throughout the world. The largest populations of Jews are located in the United States, Israel, and a number of European nations. Israelis are citizens of the modern state of Israel. Not all Israelis are religiously practicing Jews, though under Israeli law, all Jews are entitled to become Israelis.

Basic Beliefs of Judaism

Like all religions, Judaism has undergone many changes since its beginnings. Judaism, as a developed, organized religion, was born about 2,600 years ago during the period known as the Exile, when the Jews were dominated by the ancient Babylonians. Today, a number of different branches of the Jewish faith exist. Though some aspects of the religion differ, all branches of Judaism share certain basic beliefs, principles, and tenets, or truths. The first tenet of Judaism is that there is only one universal God. This God is the God not only of the Jews, but the God of all peoples and nations. This God is Yahweh, creator of the universe, believed to be eternal, perfect, all-knowing, holy, and without physical form. Yahweh is said to control nature and history, and to be greater than humans can understand or know. Yahweh is described in the Biblical book of Exodus as a just God who is merciful and compassionate but capable of great anger when his rules for moral and ethical behavior are violated.

The second tenet of Judaism is that the Jews were specially chosen by God to receive his Law. The Jews find examples of this tenet in the covenants, or agreements, that were made between God and humankind. The first covenant was God's selection of Abraham to be the father of the great nation that would live in the Promised Land of Canaan.

Now the Lord said to Abram, "Go from your country
and your kindred and your father's house to the land
that I will show you. And I will make of you a great
nation, and I will bless you, and make your name great,
so that you will be a blessing. I will bless those who
bless you, and him who curses you I will curse; and by
you all the families of the earth shall bless themselves."
(Genesis 12:1–3)

The Hebrew Bible describes numerous incidents in which God saves his people to prove his love for them and his commitment to this first covenant with Abraham. For the Jews, the more important covenant was announced later by God through Moses at Mount Sinai. There, the Law, including the Ten Commandments, was delivered to the Hebrews. This Mosaic covenant accentuated the obligation of God's chosen people to live according to the laws God revealed through Moses.

The Law is preserved in the Torah, which consists of the first five books of the Hebrew Bible. Though the different branches of Judaism differ as to how to interpret the Law, all agree that the Law is central to Jewish life. It is primarily a code of ethical behavior with two basic precepts: "Love God above all things" and "Love thy neighbor as thyself." The moral and ethical teachings of the Law demand dignified treatment of others, respect for the family, charitable works to help the sick, the poor, and the elderly, and education of the young. As the judge of the universe, Yahweh rewards those who follow his Law and punishes those who disobey.

Jewish tradition holds that prophets once acted as mediators between Yahweh and the people. These prophets were figures such as Moses, Samuel, Amos, Isaiah, Jeremiah, and Ezekiel. In the ancient nation of Israel, priests oversaw the religious rites and rituals of the land. Priests helped individuals to pray to God and to obey the Law. In modern Judaism, there is no priestly group through which individuals must communicate with God. Instead, the individual prays directly to God. The religious leaders are rabbis who are learned in the Law and who are responsible for studying, interpreting, and explaining the Law to the people.

■ **Jewish Calendar**—*The present Jewish calendar is both lunar and solar: the months are reckoned according to the moon and the years according to the sun.*

Jewish Observances—*All Jewish Holidays and the Sabbath begin at sunset of the preceding evening.*

Rosh Hashanah—*Jewish New Year: initiates religious New Year and begins a 10-day period of repentance and meditation that ends with Yom Kippur—Day of Atonement. Tishrei 1–10 (Sept–Oct)*

Sukkot—*Feast of Tabernacles: is also known as the Festival of Booths. It is symbolized by booths (Sukkot), which remind Jews of the huts in which the Israelites lived during the wilderness years. Tishrei 15–21 (Sept–Oct)*

Shemini Atzeret—*Eighth Day of the Assembly: the closing day for Sukkot that includes prayers for a good harvest for the coming year. Tishrei 22 (Sept–Oct)*

Simchat Torah—*Rejoicing with the Torah: a joyous feast when the reading cycle of the Torah is completed and its first book is begun again. Tishrei 23 (Sept–Oct)*

Hanukkah—*Feast of Lights: an eight-day celebration of the Jews' victory over the Assyrian oppression in 165 B.C.E. Kislev 25–Tevet 3 (Dec)*

Tu B'Shevat—*Jewish Arbor Day: joyous celebration of the coming of Spring. Shevat 15 (Jan–Feb)*

Purim—*Feast of Lots: a joyous holiday celebration of the rescue of the Jews of ancient Persia from a plot to destroy them. It is based on the Book of Esther. Adar 14 (Feb–Mar)*

Pesach—*Passover: a festival that commemorates the Israelite exodus from Egypt. The story is retold during a meal known as the Seder, read from a book known as the Haggadah. Nisan 15–22 (Mar–Apr)*

Yom Hashoah—*Holocaust Memorial Day: commemorates the murder of six million Jews by Hitler and the Nazi regime. Nisan 27 (May)*

Yom HaAtzmaut—*Independence Day for the State of Israel. Lyar 5 (Apr–May)*

Shavuot—*Feast of Weeks: a festival celebrating the giving of the Torah and the Commandments at Mount Sinai and the harvest of the first fruits. Sivan 6–7 (May–June)*

Tisha B'Av—*The Ninth Day of Av: a solemn day of fasting and mourning for the destruction of the first and second Temples, Jerusalem, and other tragedies of Jewish history. Av 9 (July–Aug)*

The synagogue is the center of Jewish religious, educational, and social life. The word *synagogue* comes from the Greek word meaning "assembly," and indeed, synagogues are places in which Jews assemble. In synagogues, communal prayer services are led by rabbis and cantors (special religious singers). Of special importance in the life of a synagogue are the Sabbath services and the services of a number of holy days. The most holy of days in the Jewish year are Yom Kippur (Day of Atonement), Rosh Hashanah (New Year), the Feast of Tabernacles, Purim (Feast of Lots), and Passover. Jews observe special traditions on these days to recall historical events or other important occasions. A large part of the observation of these holidays are the services and traditional meals that are celebrated in the home. Such ceremonies and celebrations reflect Judaism's strong focus on the family as a central support of Jewish religion.

A traditional Jewish belief is that a Messiah, or savior, will come to restore the Jewish nation. When this Messiah comes, those who have accepted his leadership and obeyed the Law will be rewarded, and those who have failed to obey will be punished. The Messiah will rule a perfect world. In this world, the faithful Jews, as the people of the covenant, will be a "beacon of light" through which all other nations might know God and learn his justice. According to Jewish belief, Israel will be the messianic nation, or one led by the Messiah, who will bring the whole world to worship the God of Abraham. Its citizens will adhere strictly to the Law and so make a perfectly just state. As such, Israel will be the model for the rest of the world. Certain branches of Judaism do not believe in the Messiah as the head of a theocratic, or religiously ruled, state of Israel. Rather, they believe that the Messiah will bring peace and love among all nations as an inspiring leader.

Along with its larger ethical concerns, the Law also requires observant Jews to follow certain dietary restrictions and to observe the Sabbath. Strict adherence to the Law requires that only kosher ("fitting" or "proper") food be eaten. Kosher meat includes only the meat of animals that chew their cud and have cloven hoofs. Only fish with gills and scales may be eaten. The animals and fish that provide this meat must be butchered

 *A Jewish family celebrating Seder, a feast held at the beginning of Passover and commemorating the Jews' exodus from the slavery of Egypt.*

according to special rabbinical rituals. Furthermore, milk (or milk products) and meat (or meat products) may not be eaten at the same meal. For the Passover holiday meals, special food is prepared. In the homes of those who follow kosher laws, separate plates and utensils are used to prepare and serve meat, dairy products, and Passover meals.

Jews observe the Sabbath day to remember that God rested after creating the universe. On this day, Jews who practice the religious traditions must devote themselves to prayer and study and may do no work whatsoever. Obvious forms of work include performing a job, driving a car, or traveling by other means. However, other forms of work, no matter how slight, such as lighting a match, turning on a light switch, preparing food, and the like, are also prohibited.

Today, only very traditional Jews follow every detail of the dietary and Sabbath restrictions. Some branches of modern

Judaism have relaxed these laws according to their reinterpretations of the Law. Some Jews do not observe these laws at all.

The Diaspora and Relationships with Other Communities

"I am a stranger in a foreign land," said Moses when he was in the land of Midian, south of Canaan, exiled from both Egypt and the Hebrew community that lived there. His statement epitomizes the situation of the Jews from earliest times to the present. Exile, which is separation from one's country and home, is the central theme in the traditional history of the Jews. First Abraham and his family wandered in lands that were not their own. Then the Hebrews were in bondage in Egypt. The Northern Kingdom of Israel was forced into exile by the Assyrians in 721 B.C.E. and then vanished from history. After the demise of the Southern Kingdom of Judah in 586 B.C.E., many Jews went into exile in Babylon and others fled to Egypt and elsewhere. After 538 B.C.E., some Jews, freed by the Persian king Cyrus, returned to Judah to rebuild the city of Jerusalem and restore the temple in which to worship. Others remained in the ancient territories of Babylon, Persia, and Egypt, where vibrant and influential communities existed until the 1950s. After the conquests of Alexander the Great, the Jews traveled throughout the Greek world and settled in many of the major commercial centers. When the rebuilt, or Second, Temple was destroyed in 70 C.E., some Jews migrated to Italy and then traveled the Roman trade routes into Europe, or into what are now Arab lands. Over time, small—and in many cases, thriving—Jewish communities grew up throughout Europe, particularly Eastern Europe. Later, new communities developed in the Americas. Yet the Jews were always a minority in lands not their own. This scattering of Jewish communities throughout the world is known as the Diaspora.

After the end of the independent nation of Judah (586 B.C.E.), the Jews were ruled successively by Persians, Greeks, and Romans in their own nation. Rebellions broke out when foreign rulers attempted to impose their own religion and stamp out Judaism. Judaism permits the acceptance of foreign civil law, as long as Jewish religious law is also observed. Furthermore,

friendships, commerce and business, and political interactions may be conducted with non-Jews without any restrictions. In traditional Judaism, intermarriage with non-Jews is prohibited because of its threat to the continuation of Judaism. Even in this regard, however, certain branches of modern Judaism do not enforce the rule. Therefore, as long as religious freedom is permitted, the communities of the Diaspora observe the civil laws of the nations in which they live, and they participate fully in the life of their lands.

The long history of the Jews of the Diaspora is a complex story. It is often a tale of rejection, isolation, expulsion, and persecution; but it also presents a record of cultural achievement and commercial success. In ancient times, after Alexander the Great conquered Palestine in 332 B.C.E., exiled Jews set up renowned Jewish communities in Alexandria, Egypt, and Babylonia. Alexandrian Jewish scholars translated the Pentateuch, or first five books of the Torah, into Greek. Jewish writers also produced works of literature and philosophy. In Babylonia, the exiled rabbis adapted the central tenets of the Jewish legal and theological system to the new culture. This eventually produced the Babylonian Talmud, a synthesis of Jewish written and oral law that guided Jewish life in the new surroundings, that over the years became markedly dominated by Muslim culture. When Rome took over Palestine in 63 B.C.E., the rabbis developed the Palestinian Talmud under the differing influences of Roman rule and the birth of Christianity. The Babylonian Talmud became the legal and theological quide for the Sefardic Jews in a world of Arabic-Muslim culture. Ashkenazic Jews who lived in a Latin-Christian culture followed the Palestinian Talmud developed in the Roman world.

Medieval Jews enjoyed commercial success and financial influence as traders and bankers, but experienced also a great deal of persecution and exile. They were expelled from England in 1290 C.E. and from France in 1306 C.E. In 1492 C.E., Jews in Spain were forced either to become Christians or to be expelled. However, the Marranos, or Jewish converts to Christianity, were held in suspicion by Christians; and they were also treated as traitors by Jews.

With the eighteenth century Enlightenment, Jews were emancipated. In an effort to gain full, equal citizenship many called for a reform of and updating of Jewish attitudes and values to make themselves more acceptable to the new secular culture. Modern or Reform Judaism was born in Germany and France, and was later exported to the United States. It set aside the old ways of Orthodoxy. Conservative Judaism tried to attain a middle ground: accepting many reform issues but also keeping traditional religious observances.

After the extermination of millions of European Jews during the Nazi Holocaust of World War II, the establishment of the state of Israel in 1948 once again created a Jewish nation to which all members of the Diaspora were invited to return. Israel became a haven for Jews fleeing religious persecution and those seeking a homeland of their own. However, the well-established communities of the Diaspora remained in place. Some believe that these communities must continue to exist if Israel is to survive. Furthermore, ultra-Orthodox Jews do not believe that Israel is the true Jewish religious state because, according to their belief, such a nation will exist only with the coming of the Messiah.

Judaism and the Jews Today

Judaism has grown throughout its many years to include a number of different branches of the faith. Throughout the world, communities of Jews who are also citizens of the lands in which they live practice their particular branch of Judaism. The nation of Israel is the Jewish homeland. Israel is not a re-creation of the state of ancient Israel. Instead, its citizens include members of the various branches of Judaism, as well as non-Jews.

The Diaspora has given rise to a unique, worldwide Jewish culture that includes, but is not limited to, religious observance. This culture was shaped by the Jews being forced to live in close communities among people with different ideas about the world. Jewish culture embodies the values of the Law involving community service and education. It also maintains a deep respect for tradition. From this culture comes a vast

body of music, art, and literature, ranging from philosophical analyses to humor, all of which reflect the Jewish response to the world.

Jews today include members of the branches of Judaism as well as people who are culturally Jewish. Some Jews are observant members of the traditional faith, still living in very close communities centered around the synagogue. Far more are followers of other branches of Judaism that have been shaped by the changing world in which the Jews have lived. Other Jews do not practice Judaism at all. Instead, because of their family backgrounds, they have inherited the Jewish culture of the Diaspora. When considering Judaism and the Jews, then, one must think not only in terms of a religious tradition but also in terms of a specific culture. Both have had an extraordinary influence on Western civilization.

2

Early History of the Jews and Judaism

*A*ccording to the Biblical account, early Judaism is a story of promises, faith, devotion, persecution, and wandering. God's early promises to the Jews formed the lasting core of their religion. Faith in God's plan for them and devotion to his Law held the Jews together through times of peace, war, slavery, and suffering.

Sources

Until the middle of the nineteenth century C.E. (common era or Christian era, also known as A.D.), most of what we knew about early Judaism was learned from the Hebrew Bible. The Hebrew Bible, with some revisions and reordering of the texts, is the basis for the Old Testament of the Christian Bible. The New Testament of the Christian Bible also provides some of the history of Judaism and its people. Additional information comes from classical (Greek and Roman) sources and early Jewish non-Biblical writings. Archaeological explorations begun in the nineteenth century in the Near East have provided new evidence from remnants of cities and towns, personal belongings, literature, and other relics. Artifacts from Mesopotamia, Egypt, Syria,

Preceding page-
The Temple area in
Jerusalem is filled with
worshipers during the
high holy days.

Turkey, and the Holy Land (also called Palestine, Syria-Palestine, Canaan, or Israel) have told us much more about the neighbors of the Hebrews and the Israelites. Together, the Hebrew Bible and the archaeological discoveries have helped to form a clearer picture of the probable origins of the Hebrews and the faith that united them. While much progress has been made in these areas of study, Biblical scholarship is a continuing process of careful research that is constantly being refined as new information emerges.

Ancestry and Language

The precise origin of the Hebrew people and their descendants, the Israelites, is not known. The Bible links the Hebrews' ancestry to that of all people on earth through Noah, who built the ark to save his family from the Flood. With Noah's sons, Shem, Ham, and Japheth, the genealogical lines of the nations separate. Shem, whose family included Eber, was the ancestor of the Hebrews and certain Mesopotamian, Syrian, and Arabian peoples. Elsewhere in the Bible, the Aramaeans, an ancient people of present-day Syria, are named as the ancestors of the Hebrews: "A wandering Aramaean was my father," said the Israelite in Deuteronomy 26:5. However, in Genesis, the Bible also refers to the Hebrews' kinship with Arab tribes (through Ishmael, Abraham's first son) and the ancient Near Eastern peoples of Moab, Ammon, and Edom. These references suggest that the Hebrews originated in the region extending from Syria to the borders of Egypt and were related to the other peoples of the area.

The evidence of the Hebrew language supports this idea. The Hebrew language is the language of ancient Israel and of the Old Testament. It is related to Aramaic, Arabic, and a number of ancient languages such as Akkadian (the language of Babylon and Assyria), Ugaritic, and Phoenician. These are languages of Mesopotamia, Syria, and Arabia. We call all of these languages "Semitic" languages (from the name of Noah's son Shem). Their speakers were and are Semitic people. Hebrew is a Semitic language, and the Jews are considered to be a Semitic people.

The Bible identifies the people descended from Jacob, one of the patriarchs who was also called Israel, as the "children of

Israel." The Biblical account describes the development of these people from a large extended family to a nation that settled in Canaan. Archaeological evidence indicates that there was a people called "Israel" in Canaan in the late second millennium B.C.E. Further, many scholars believe that a new people entered Canaan at around the time described in the Bible. This new people joined with existing inhabitants of Canaan to form the group known as Israel.

The Patriarchs

According to the Bible, the first patriarch, or father, of the Hebrews was Abraham. God made a covenant with Abraham, promising that a great nation with its home in Canaan would descend from him. The patriarchal narratives of the Bible (Genesis 12–50) relate events in the lives of four generations of patriarchs. These early fathers were Abraham, his son Isaac, Isaac's son Jacob, eleven of Jacob's twelve sons, and the sons of Joseph, Jacob's favorite son.

The patriarch Abraham is described as a nomad who wandered from Ur in Chaldea, through Syria and Canaan to Egypt, and then back to Canaan. He led a tribe that moved with the seasons in search of pasture for its flocks. The Biblical book of Genesis describes the nomadic lives of Abraham and the other patriarchs and tells how they interacted with peoples settled throughout the lands where they wandered. Many other ancient Near Eastern sources tell of tribes that were like the early Hebrews. Among these sources are documents from the site of Mari (in Syria) from the first half of the second millennium B.C.E. These documents describe interaction with settlers who were similar to those portrayed in Genesis.

In the Bible, the patriarchal narratives include details about issues such as marriage, inheritance, relations with other tribes or nations, the herding of livestock, and the acquisition of real estate. From these stories, we gain insight into the social and economic environment of the Hebrews. In comparing them with neighboring tribes, we also learn about their legal practices, which were generally the same as those of other ancient Near Eastern societies, especially those in Mesopotamia.

The Hebrew Alphabet	
Name	Type
aleph	א
veth (beth)	ב ב
gimel	ג
daleth	ד
he	ה
vav	ו
zayin	ז
heth	ח
teth	ט
yod	י
khaph (kaph)	כ כ ך
lamed	ל
mem	מ ם
nun	נ ן
samekh	ס
ayin	ע
feh (peh)	פ פ ף
tsadi	צ ץ
koph	ק
resh	ר
shin (sin)	ש ש
tav	ת

The early religion of the Hebrews is also reflected in the patriarchal narratives. We know from these stories that the God of the early Hebrews was the patron, or guardian, of the family. God is called Yahweh in the patriarchal narratives, but the favored name for God is 'El. 'El is usually used in combination with other words such as 'El Shaddai, 'El Elyon, and 'El Olam. These words give the name of God more specific meaning. 'El Shaddai, for example, means "God of the Mountain," 'El Elyon means, "God Most High," and 'El Olam means "Everlasting God." Because 'El is the Semitic term for "god," all these names that include 'El may simply describe the one god of the Patriarchs. The chief deity of ancient Canaan before the arrival of Abraham was also called 'El, and the relationship between this god and the names for the Hebrews' God is not clear. We do know that the 'El of the Hebrews and that of the Canaanites were not identical in character. It is important to note that since about the third century B.C.E., the pronunciation of Yahweh has been avoided by Jewish people, to show respect for the majesty of God. Though references to Yahweh are often found in textbooks and encyclopedias, in religious contexts the word Adonai, meaning "Lord" is generally substituted. Another alternative to express this reverence is to use the form G-d.

As far as worship was concerned, early Hebrew practices were simple, as necessitated by a nomadic way of life. Animal sacrifices were conducted by the head of the family, and people offered personal prayers to God. The early Hebrews, like their patriarch, Abraham, believed in their covenant with God and the divine promises made to them.

Scholars debate the time of the Age of the Patriarchs. Some believe that these early fathers lived in the Middle Bronze Age (circa 2000–1550 B.C.E.). Others think that they lived in the Late Bronze Age (circa 1500–1200 B.C.E.). Though they disagree about the time, both of these groups believe that the stories of the patriarchs were passed on by word of mouth and then eventually committed to writing. A third group of scholars believes that the stories originated and were written down at the same time. All of these scholars, however, believe that the narratives were written down in the first millennium B.C.E.

Exodus to the Conquest

Egyptian literature has many stories of nomadic herdsmen migrating to Egypt during troubled times in Canaan. Historical evidence makes it likely that this was the experience of at least some of the tribes that were to become the Israelites. A date for this migration, however, has not been agreed upon. In the Bible, the end of the patriarchal narratives finds the descendants of Abraham dwelling in Egypt. They, like the nomads of Egyptian records, had moved to Egypt because of a famine in Canaan.

The traditional Biblical story states that the Hebrews were enslaved in Egypt for four hundred years. According to the book of Exodus in the Bible, the Hebrews moved away from Egypt during the reign of a pharaoh who can be identified as Rameses II (1290–1224 B.C.E.). There is no mention of this event in Egyptian historical records, perhaps because it was fairly common for a small number of Asiatic peoples to depart from the Egyptian Delta. Nonetheless, the Jews recount their departure from Egypt as the Exodus, recorded as one of the major events in Hebrew history. This liberation from slavery in Egypt was an enormous victory for the Jews, and a turning point in Hebrew religion.

It is believed that during the Exodus, the great leader Moses brought the Hebrews from Egypt to Mount Sinai. There, one of the most sacred events of Jewish history occurred—Moses received the Law from God and gave it to the Hebrews.

> And God spoke all these words, saying, "I am the Lord your God, Who brought you out of the land of Egypt, out of the house of bondage.
>
> "You shall have no other gods before Me.
>
> "You shall not make for yourself a graven image, or any likeness of anything that is in heaven above, or that is in the earth beneath, or that is in the water under the earth; you shall not bow down to them or serve them, for I the Lord your God am a jealous God, visiting the iniquity of the fathers upon the children to the third and the fourth generation of those who hate Me, but showing

steadfast love to thousands of those who love Me and keep My commandments.

"You shall not take the name of the Lord your God in vain; for the Lord will not hold him guiltless who takes His name in vain.

"Remember the sabbath day, to keep it holy. Six days you shall labor, and do all your work; but the seventh day is a sabbath to the Lord your God; in it you shall not do any work, you, or your son, or your daughter, your manservant, or your maidservant, or your cattle, or the sojourner who is within your gates; for in six days the Lord made heaven and earth, the sea, and all that is in them, and rested the seventh day; therefore the Lord blessed the sabbath day and hallowed it.

"Honor your father and your mother, that your days may be long in the land which the Lord your God gives you.

"You shall not kill.

"You shall not commit adultery.

"You shall not steal.

"You shall not bear false witness against your neighbor.

"You shall not covet your neighbor's house; you shall not covet your neighbor's wife, or his manservant, or his maidservant, or his ox, or his ass, or anything that is your neighbor's." (Exodus 20:1–17)

After receiving the divine Law, the Israelites wandered in the wilderness for forty years. This period of wandering is known as the Wilderness Experience. At the end of the forty years, the Israelites, led by Joshua, Moses' successor, entered the land of Canaan, where they had lived centuries earlier. Once they were in the land of Canaan, the Israelites conquered it. This period is known as the Conquest.

Archaeological evidence concerning the name *Israel* and the conquest of Israel presents a somewhat different picture. The

■ *This etching of Moses Breaking the Tables of the Law reenacts the scene of Exodus 32:19, when Moses accuses his fellow Jews of breaking their covenant with God.*

oldest outside reference to the Israelites comes from Egypt. The pharaoh Merneptah (circa 1220 B.C.E.) in Canaan described his military campaigns on a stone stela (monument) and stated that Israel was "utterly destroyed." This "Israel" was already in Canaan before the time associated with the Exodus.

The Israelites who settled in Canaan had very different religious, social, legal, political, and economic lives from the Hebrews of the patriarchal era, because many ideas and practices

changed during the forty years of the Wilderness Experience and the period of conquest and settlement. New perspectives from the periods of the Exodus and the Conquest played an important role in forming Judaism and the way of life in ancient Israel.

The Biblical account of Exodus describes the development of many of Israel's unique national characteristics. The Israelites changed socially and politically after the Conquest and settlement. They were no longer a nomadic people. They settled in villages and farmed the land. In the Bible, the twelve tribes of Israel were described as a family before the Conquest, because they had the same father, Jacob (Israel). Each tribe considered the others to be family. But, after settling in Canaan, the Israelites were loosely organized as a league, or group, of tribes. The Israelites no longer thought it important for the tribes to be related as family. More important was the tribes' common religion and their former agreement to defend each other in times of trouble. Now, the tribal league did not have a central government. The Biblical record shows that after the Conquest, the tribes enjoyed a good deal of autonomy, though at times the leaders and elders met and legislated for the entire people.

The most important change occurred in religion. The Israelites had only one God, Yahweh, and they considered the many names used by the Hebrews of the patriarchal era for their God, ('El Shaddai, 'El Elyon, 'El Olam) as different names for Yahweh. According to the Biblical book of Joshua, the Israelites renewed their covenant with Yahweh.

> Then Joshua gathered all the tribes of Israel to Shechem, and summoned the elders, the heads, the judges, and the officers of Israel; and they presented themselves before God.

> And Joshua said to all the people, "Thus says the Lord, the God of Israel, 'Your fathers lived of old beyond the Euphrates, even Terah, the father of Abraham and of Nahor; and they served other gods.

> 'Then I took your father Abraham from beyond the river and led him through all the land of Canaan, and made his offspring many. I gave him Isaac.

■ **Twelve Tribes of Israel** (or Jacob) are indicated in Genesis 36:22–26:

Reuben	Dan
Simeon	Naphtali
Levi	Gad
Judah	Asher
Issachar	Joseph
Zebulun	Benjamin

'And to Isaac I gave Jacob and Esau. And I gave Esau the hill country of Seir to possess, but Jacob and his children went down to Egypt.

'And I sent Moses and Aaron, and I plagued Egypt with what I did in the midst of it; and afterwards I brought you out.

'Then I brought your fathers out of Egypt, and you came to the sea; and the Egyptians pursued your fathers with chariots and horsemen to the Red Sea.

'And when they cried to the Lord, He put darkness between you and the Egyptians, and made the sea come upon them and cover them; and your eyes saw what I did to Egypt; and you lived in the wilderness a long time.

'Then I brought you to the land of the Amorites, who lived on the other side of the Jordan; they fought with you, and I gave them into your hand, and you took possession of their land, and I destroyed them before you.'"

But Joshua said to the people, "You cannot serve the Lord; for He is a holy God; He is a jealous God; He will not forgive your transgressions or your sins.

"If you forsake the Lord and serve foreign gods, then He will turn and do you harm, and consume you, after having done you good."

And the people said to Joshua, "The Lord our God we will serve, and His voice we will obey."
    (Joshua 24:1–8; 19–20, 24)

The Israelites worshiped God directly. They were forbidden to worship any image, statue, or other material likeness of Yahweh. Such worship of idols was common in the ancient Near East. Another difference between Yahweh and the gods of other ancient Near Eastern peoples was that Yahweh was not associated with any one particular place as were the local and national deities of the era. Yet another difference was that Yahweh was

not associated with any one part of nature (such as the sea, a wind storm, or earth). In this respect, Yahweh was a unique deity in antiquity.

In the town of Shiloh, Yahweh was worshiped in a central place. In a shrine they kept a sacred box called the Ark of the Covenant, which held the tablets that contained the Ten Commandments, said to have been given to Moses by God at Mount Sinai. Thus, the Ark of the Covenant was considered very holy. Both Biblical tradition and archaeological evidence indicate that the original shrine for the Ark was a tent, "The Tabernacle." This type of portable shrine well served the needs of a nomadic people. Worship of Yahweh was regulated by a high priest along with some lesser priests and servants who belonged to the tribe of Levi (a son of Jacob). Animal sacrifices played a role in worship, but more important were the annual feasts such as Passover and the Feast of Weeks. During these feasts, believers gathered and reaffirmed the covenant between Israel and Yahweh.

■ *Three artistic representations of Hebrew priests: a Levite, a Kohen, and a high priest.*

The Law that Moses received at Mount Sinai gave the terms of the covenant between God and Israel. The Israelites believed that the Law, because it was given by God, was eternal, universal, and holy. A part of the Law, the Ten Commandments, set general guidelines for the worship of God and interaction among people. There were also many specific laws; concrete applications of the basic principles of the Ten Commandments. These laws were similar to those of other ancient Near Eastern law codes. These concrete applications, or case laws, reflect how the Israelites adapted to the norms of settled life in the ancient Near East.

Central to belief in Yahweh were two ideas: the Israelites were Yahweh's chosen people, and the covenant at Mount Sinai made Israel into a nation. Yahweh was the divine king who defended Yahweh's chosen people, Israel, and provided for its other needs. In other lands, the laws were made by human kings. The unique feature of Israelite law was that it had a divine origin—it was created by Yahweh. Therefore, the social, economic, and legal foundations of Israel were also divinely ordained. The people of Israel tried to live according to Yahweh's Law as it had been received at Mount Sinai. The human leader of Israel was a judge who oversaw the divine Law and mediated between Yahweh and his people in every area of activity.

For those outside Judaism, the question remains: Why and how did Judaism come to hold these unique perspectives concerning the divine and its relationship to the human? In the Bible, the answer is found in the story of Moses and the Hebrews at Mount Sinai. There, the Hebrews received God's word directly through Moses and thus established a personal relationship with God. The Bible also remembers Moses as the greatest of the nation's leaders. Indeed, the figure of Moses dominates the human side of the story of the Wilderness. He was called by Yahweh, led the people out of Egypt, received the Law, and intervened with Yahweh on behalf of the wayward people. The rich stories concerning Moses reflect the fact that he was a charismatic leader, credited as the divine instrument and human founder of a new and unique faith. He ranks with Jesus and Muhammad in the history of great religious prophets.

The Period of the Judges

The period of the Exodus, the Conquest, and settlement was one of general instability in the ancient Near East. The great empires of the second millennium B.C.E., such as those of the Egyptians, the Hittites, and the Assyrians, withdrew from their traditional spheres of influence in Syria and Canaan. This left a political and military vacuum that was filled by new peoples. Phoenicians developed the cities in the northern coastal areas. Aramaeans spread into Syria and northern and eastern Canaan. The Israelites and the Philistines, among others, occupied the southern and western areas of Canaan. Within this environment, Israel continued its development as a nation. The Israelites settled in Canaan, and Israel entered the so-called Period of the Judges (circa 1200–1020 B.C.E.).

As previously mentioned, Israel around 1200 B.C.E. was organized as a tribal league. During the Period of the Judges, geographical factors, such as the distance between tribal territories and the features of the land, led to disunity among the tribes. Local political and military problems and local worship of God were of greater interest to the tribes than larger, common issues. Still, the tradition of the Covenant and its requirements seems to have held the tribes together, although rather loosely. In keeping with the tradition of the Wilderness era, the leader in times of emergency was a judge whose charisma persuaded people to follow him. Among the best known judges were Othniel, Ehud, Gideon, Deborah, Jepthah, and Samson. These judges had very different backgrounds, but all appear to have been inspired in their leadership and saved at least a part of Israel from its enemies.

This period was one of economic and technological advances for Israel. As Israel came into closer contact with other cultures, its people acquired new knowledge and skills. From the Philistines, who at first dominated them by their use of iron weapons and agricultural implements, the Israelites eventually learned the art of smelting metal to form new kinds of spears and tools. The Israelites also encountered other religions, especially the cults of Ba'al, the chief deity of Canaan. Ba'al was a pagan god whose followers worshiped idols. For the Israelites and the people around them, a long-lived tension arose regarding the

worship of Yahweh and the worship of pagan gods. This tension put pressure on the Israelites to define their religious and political identity. It is to the Period of the Judges that the "identity problem" of ancient Israel can be traced.

Again, the Hebrew Bible, especially the book of Judges, is almost the only written record of this era. The book of Judges views this period as one marked by alternating times of crisis and peace, and establishes the moral message that loyalty to God brings peace and that disloyalty is a guarantee of disaster.

The United Monarchy

In the wake of turmoil at the end of the second millennium B.C.E. (circa 1100–1000 B.C.E.), the traditional bases of power in the Near East—Egypt, Mesopotamia, and Turkey—were reorganizing. With no strong opponent in the region, Israel ultimately became the dominant power in Canaan. Before that happened, however, changes occurred in Israel's structure. The history of the Israelites entered the Period of Monarchy.

Again, the Biblical record—especially I and II Samuel, I Kings, and I Chronicles—is the only written source for the early events of the Period of Monarchy. These portions of the Hebrew Bible contain many stories about principal figures and are highly literary in character. A picture of the emergence of the monarchy in ancient Israel comes from a vast amount of scholarly investigation of both archaeological findings and patterns of political history.

The Biblical account presents the birth of the Monarchy in the following way. During the rule of Samuel, Israel's last judge, the people asked for a king to lead them in battle and save them from their enemies. They said, "No! but we will have a king over us, that we also may be like all the nations, and that our king may govern us and go out before us and fight our battles," (Samuel 8:19–20). Yahweh thought this demand was a rejection of his rule as king. However, He gave the people a king named Saul. Saul ruled, and the judge Samuel maintained his role as a link to God. Saul had some success in battle, but he had poor judgment and disobeyed Yahweh when he clashed with Samuel in certain critical situations. Yahweh eventually withdrew his

favor from Saul and instructed Samuel to anoint David as the next king of Israel. Saul met his end in a battle with the Philistines.

Most scholars believe that Israel became a kingship when the Israelites found that the loosely organized tribal confederation was not adequate to provide for Israel's defense and growth. Israel was apparently influenced by neighboring nations that had kingships, and they adopted these other local models of government as their own. According to this theory, the figures of Samuel and Saul represent the tensions between the old and the new ways. The reign of Saul (circa 1020–1000 B.C.E.) marks the period of change between the ways.

David (circa 1000–961 B.C.E.), the second king selected by God, ranks second only to Moses in Biblical tradition. Whereas Moses was the founder of the Israel of the Wilderness Era, David was the founder of the Monarchy, Israel's form of government at the height of its power and independence. The stories about David in the Hebrew Bible are the stuff of legend. In one story, he is presented as a brave shepherd-boy who defeats the Philistine giant Goliath. He is also portrayed as a supremely talented musician, a kind of Biblical Robin Hood, and the king whom Yahweh confirmed through the Covenant of Kingship as the first member of the dynasty of Israel's kings. According to the Bible, David became king after eluding Saul's insane pursuit of him. He demonstrated his love for and obedience to God, and he won the hearts of the people through his loyalty and heroism. Of special importance, his campaigns extended Israelite territory roughly to that promised by God in the Covenant of Abraham—from the Euphrates River to the border of Egypt. With David's reign, God's promise to Abraham that he would give to him and his descendants all the land of Canaan was fulfilled.

In many respects, David resembles the judges in that he was a charismatic leader with great force of personality. As one reads through the stories of the Bible, one might understand David to be a politically astute individual who was able to control the internal and external forces affecting Israel and so gain control of the Monarchy. Early in his career, he began to shape

the workings of the kingship of Israel and the structure of the court so that he ruled through a more formal organization than that of Saul. He made a series of treaties with neighboring nations to assure peace where possible. Through his military expeditions, he extended Israel's territory significantly. He also captured Jerusalem and made it the governmental and religious

■ *The young David, future King of all Israel, fights the Philistine giant, Goliath, in this etching that portrays* **I Samuel 17**.

center for Israel. There is no evidence concerning David's accomplishments beyond the stories recounted in the Hebrew Bible. There is also very little evidence of the practices of Israelite kingship and its religious nature, outside the Biblical sources. However, it is clear that there was a period of political consolidation at the beginning of the Monarchy under Saul and David and that the general structure of Israel's kingship was established at that time.

The Davidic Covenant, or Covenant of Kingship, which established David as a king distinct from Yawheh (the traditional king), led to religious and social tensions among the Israelites. The Bible declares that God made a covenant with David, whereby David would be the head of an eternal dynasty of Israel. David and his descendants were obligated to follow the Law lest the king and the nation suffer.

> *The God of Israel has spoken, the Rock of Israel has said to me: When one rules justly over men, ruling in the fear of God,*
>
> *He dawns on them like the morning light, like the sun shining forth upon a cloudless morning, like rain that makes grass to sprout from the earth.*
>
> *Yea, does not my house stand so with God? For He has made with me an everlasting covenant, ordered in all things and secure.* (II Samuel 23:3–5)

The covenant made with David was similar to the one made with Abraham in that it was an absolute promise. However, the Davidic Covenant altered certain elements of the covenant at Mount Sinai. This was where the tension arose. The most noticeable difference was that the covenant at Mount Sinai declared that Yahweh was king. The Davidic Covenant declared that David was king. This basic difference led to two ideals of Israelite organization. While many Israelites accepted the rule of David, some could not, because they felt that only Yahweh was the king. Though the Davidic Covenant became the official standard for Israel, this difference between the two covenants continued to cause tensions throughout the Monarchy.

It was during the period of David's kingship that the city of Jerusalem became the center of Israelite government and religion. Until David's reign, Jerusalem was held by the Jebusites, a people of Canaan. Over time, especially as the Monarchy declined, Jerusalem became the symbol of God's promise to Israel and the center for Israel's hope for the future. To this day, Jews of the Diaspora say, "Next year may we be in Jerusalem," at the Passover celebration.

Another development associated with kingship in Israel involved the role of the prophet. The prophet was an individual called by God to communicate his will to the king and the people. The prophet's relationship to the king depended largely on the degree to which the king obeyed God and adhered to the laws of the covenant. In the stories of the early kingship, Saul and his prophet Samuel were at odds with one another. David, on the other hand, had a "court prophet," Nathan. Nathan announced God's covenant to David, chastised David when he went astray, and advised him on many matters. These stories reflect how the prophets behaved during much of the Monarchy and beyond.

After David, Israel was ruled by his son, Solomon. Solomon's reign (circa 961–922 B.C.E.) is described in the Bible as the peak of Israel's national achievement. Archaeological findings confirm that this was a time of flowering Israelite prosperity and culture. Israel's commerce expanded to include shipping on the Red Sea and caravan trade in horses, chariots, and pepper with Egypt and Arabia. Most importantly, Solomon is credited with building the Temple of Yahweh in Jerusalem and organizing its personnel. This temple is known as Solomon's Temple, or the First Temple of Jerusalem. Fortress cities were also strengthened and manned by permanent garrisons.

Throughout the Bible there are criticisms of Solomon's luxurious way of life and the controlling measures he took to achieve it. The Bible also points disapprovingly to Solomon's weakness for women who seductively led him to the worship of foreign gods and ultimately to his failure as king. On the other hand, Solomon was noted for his wisdom. Hence the modern phrases "as wise as Solomon," "a Solomonic decision," and the

like. Solomon also made a significant impact beyond Israel. The legendary Suleiman of the Islamic world traces his origins to Solomon of the Hebrew Bible. Ethiopian legend claims that King Solomon and the Queen of Sheba were the parents of the first Ethiopian monarch. Solomon is truly a complex character, both in history and in legend.

With Solomon's reign, the Monarchy was firmly established as Israel's form of government. In addition, Jerusalem was secured as the center of political and religious authority. The power of the Monarchy and of Jerusalem strained the local ways of the old tribal league. One particular example of this was that Solomon's system of taxation was resented in the tribal areas that had so recently been independent. After Solomon's death, these tensions became more concrete. Israel split into two nations: Israel, composed of the ten northern tribes, and Judah, retaining Jerusalem and the two southern tribes.

The Divided Monarchy

Throughout the Divided Monarchy, neither Israel nor Judah ever regained the strength or wealth of the united kingdom of Solomon's era. Instead, the two kingdoms joined in the interactions among a number of Phoenician, Philistine, and Aramaean city-states. Israel and Judah were alternately enemies and allies in the complex military, economic, and political patterns of the time. Both nations were increasingly influenced by foreign elements, especially concerning religious ideas. Both nations had to struggle with their identities in the face of foreign powers that were stronger than they were.

The Biblical books of Kings and Chronicles, along with various texts of the prophets, describe the histories of the Northern Kingdom of Israel and the Southern Kingdom of Judah from the death of Solomon until the Exile (586 B.C.E.). Each Biblical text has a particular slant, so the reports are not evenly weighted. For certain eras of the Divided Monarchy, the Biblical material can be supplemented with other ancient Near Eastern sources, particularly the records of the kings of Assyria and archaeological evidence.

In the Bible, the reigns of the kings of Israel and Judah are presented in chronological order. Because these stories come

■ Kings of Southern Kingdom of Judah	
Rehoboam	922–915
Abijah	915–913
Asa	913–873
Jehoshaphat	873–849
Jehoram	849–842
Ahaziah	842
Athaliah	842–837
Joash	837–800
Amaziah	800–783
Uzziah	783–742
Jotham	742–735
Jehoahaz I	735–715
Hezekiah	715–687
Manasseh	687–642
Amon	642–640
Josiah	640–609
Jehoahaz II	609
Johoiakim	609–598
Jeconiah	598–597
Zedekiah	597–587

from Judah, there is strong anti-Israel feeling throughout. Also, the Bible stories were written in an era when the Monarchy was blamed in part for Israel's downfall. The history of the Monarchy, therefore, is told as a sequence of kings, some of whom were faithful to Yahweh, but most of whom strayed from the Law and the correct worship of God. Among the more famous kings of Israel were Jeroboam I, who founded the kingdom of Israel and is cited throughout the Bible as the model of disloyalty to Yahweh; Ahab, son of Omri and the husband of Jezebel, against whom Elijah prophesied; and Jehu, the brutal army commander who gained power by the support of the mutinous army and who decapitated all the sons of Ahab who could have claimed the throne.

The kings of the Northern Kingdom of Israel strayed from the political and religious ideals of the Davidic Covenant. The tribes that made up Israel, from the Judahite perspective, were doomed from the start—they did not descend from David and they did not worship Yahweh in Jerusalem but worshiped instead at Bethel, Shechem, and their new capital, Samaria. The prophets from Judah were active in Israel, opposing the kings and preaching God's promise of punishment for the unfaithful. In the end, the Northern Kingdom of Israel was captured by the Assyrians. Its people were forced into exile in 722–721 B.C.E. At that point, the ten northern tribes were dispersed throughout the Assyrian empire and lost their Israelite identity.

> Then the king of Assyria invaded all the land and came to Samaria, and for three years he besieged it.
>
> In the ninth year of Hoshea the king of Assyria captured Samaria, and he carried the Israelites away to Assyria, and placed them in Halah, and in Habor, by the river of Gozan, and in the cities of the Medes.
>
> And this was so, because the people of Israel had sinned against the Lord their God, Who had brought them up out of the land of Egypt from under the hand of Pharaoh king of Egypt, and had feared other gods and walked in the customs of the nations whom the Lord drove out

Kings of Northern Kingdom of Israel	
Jeroboam I	922–901
Nadab	901–900
Baasha	900–877
Elah	877–876
Zimri	876
Omri	876–869
Ahab	869–850
Ahaziah	850–849
Jehoram	849–842
Jehu	842–815
Joahaz	815–801
Jehoash	801–786
Jeroboam II	786–746
Zechariah	746–745
Shallum	745
Menahem	745–738
Pekahiah	738–737
Pekah	737–732
Hoshea	732–724

before the people of Israel, and in the customs which the kings of Israel had introduced.

And the people of Israel did secretly against the Lord their God things that were not right. They built for themselves high places at all their towns, from watch-tower to fortified city;

They set up for themselves pillars and Asherim on every high hill and under every green tree;

And there they burned incense on all the high places, as the nations did whom the Lord carried away before them. And they did wicked things, provoking the Lord to anger,

And they served idols, of which the Lord had said to them, "You shall not do this."

Yet the Lord warned Israel and Judah by every prophet and every seer, saying, "Turn from your evil ways and keep My commandments and My statutes, in accordance with all the law which I commanded your fathers, and which I sent to you by My servants the prophets."

But they would not listen, but were stubborn, as their fathers had been, who did not believe in the Lord their God.

They despised His statutes, and His covenant that He made with their fathers, and the warnings which He gave them. They went after false idols, and became false, and they followed the nations that were round about them, concerning whom the Lord had commanded them that they should not do like them.

And they forsook all the commandments of the Lord their God, and made for themselves molten images of two calves; and they made an Asherah, and worshiped all the host of heaven, and served Ba'al.

And they burned their sons and their daughters as offerings, and used divination and sorcery, and sold

*themselves to do evil in the sight of the Lord, provoking
Him to anger.*

*Therefore the Lord was very angry with Israel, and
removed them out of His sight; none was left but the
tribe of Judah only.* (II Kings 17:5–18)

Non-Biblical sources indicate that Israel was the more powerful of the two kingdoms. Based on excavations in Samaria, we know that Israel was prosperous and that it enjoyed a high cultural life. From Assyrian sources, we know that the House of Omri was a formidable military foe. Its defeat was worthy of mention on a monument of Assyrian king Shalmaneser III. Though it was mighty, Israel was conquered by the much mightier Assyrians. We also know from Assyrian sources that it was imperial policy to deport conquered peoples and to disperse them in order to prevent any united uprising. Our knowledge of this policy confirms the Biblical stories of Israel's destruction and the dispersion of the tribes.

Judah, the smaller of the two nations, continued until 586 B.C.E. The history of the kings of Judah is the story of Yahweh's patience with his people and devotion to the promise of the Davidic Covenant. The Bible tells of Judahite kings such as Asa, Hezekiah, and Josiah, who ruled in the style of King David. It also portrays other Judahite kings, such as Rehoboam, Jehoram, Ahaz, and Manasseh, who failed to obey the divine Law. Each king's success was measured by his efforts to rid the land of pagan practices like worship of the Canaanite gods Ba'al and Asherah. In the end, God's patience with Judah ended. He punished Judah with the Exile, when it was conquered by the Babylonians.

*Judah also did not keep the commandments of the Lord
their God, but walked in the customs which Israel had
introduced.*

*And the Lord rejected all the descendants of Israel and
afflicted them, and gave them into the hand of spoilers,
until He had cast them out of His sight.*
(II Kings 17:19–20)

Archaeological findings show that Canaanite gods were worshiped in Judah and that Judah had regular contact with surrounding nations. We also know that in Judah there were periods of prosperity, such as those of the righteous kings mentioned in the Bible. Hezekiah, for example, was a model king who was said to have enjoyed great favor from God. The building projects of Hezekiah are known from archaeological excavations. It is clear that these projects were undertaken during a period of active trade and general well-being. Judah's strength under Hezekiah was confirmed by Assyrian king Sennacherib. He devoted a section of his reports, written on a clay prism, to the siege of Jerusalem, an event that is central to the Hezekiah story in the Hebrew Bible. Other excavations reveal Assyrian, Egyptian, and Babylonian presence in Judah in the form of forts and garrisons, pottery, and a large variety of artifacts.

■ *The Temple area in Jerusalem shows the Muslim Dome of the Rock that was built on the site of the old Temple in the seventh century.*

Historically, Judah was smaller than Israel and less important on the international scene. When Israel fell, Judah became a vassal state of Assyria, but later Judahite kings would proclaim their independence. Judah was caught between the powers of Assyria and Egypt and attempted to play these nations against each other. It was somewhat successful; Judah remained intact for as long as Assyria existed. When Assyria collapsed, Babylon took its place as the Mesopotamian power. Judah became the crossroads of the Babylonian and Egyptian armies clashing for supremacy in Canaan. In 587 B.C.E., when Judah refused to surrender to the Babylonian king Nebuchadnezzar, Solomon's Temple and Jerusalem were destroyed. Its leaders, craftsmen, and much of the population were deported, as Israel had been by the Assyrians. This was the beginning of the Babylonian Exile and the end of independence for ancient Israel.

In the history of Judaism, the period of the Divided Monarchy is especially important because of the prophets who were active in Israel and Judah. Like Samuel and Nathan, prophets arose in Israel and Judah to express God's displeasure with the king and the people.

The written works of the prophets reflect an Israel that was quite different from the Israel of the period of the conquest and settlement. Both Israel and Judah had major cities with people of widely differing social and economic classes and refined attitudes toward religion and politics. There were strict Yahwists and those who practiced some kind of Yahwism, side by side with worshipers of pagan gods. As the fortunes of Israel and Judah declined, people questioned how their situation related to God's promises of a land, a king, and a special place among nations.

The prophets objected strenuously to the social, economic, political, and religious conditions in Israel and Judah. They preached against the injustices of social and economic inequalities and against the abuse of authority by the wealthy and powerful. The prophets felt that Israel and Judah should not have had alliances with other nations and vassal arrangements with Assyria. They believed that these foreign affairs showed a lack of faith in the overlordship of God and his promise of protection. They were especially angered by the worship of foreign gods

and the lack of action on the part of many of the kings to abolish pagan practices. In general, they preached that Israel, Judah, and their kings had violated the covenants on which the nation was founded. The prophets interpreted the historical and environmental events of their times (the Assyrian invasions, the Exile of Israel, and earthquakes and droughts, for example) as manifestations of God's anger and his punishment for violations of the covenants. Along with their messages of doom for the nations, the prophets presented the idea that a "faithful remnant" would be saved by God to continue his grand design for Israel.

> In that day the remnant of Israel and the survivors of the house of Jacob will no more lean upon him that smote them, but will lean upon the Lord, the Holy One of Israel, in truth.
>
> A remnant will return, the remnant of Jacob, to the mighty God.
>
> For though your people Israel be as the sand of the sea, only a remnant of them will return. Destruction is decreed, overflowing with righteousness.
>
> For the Lord, the Lord of hosts, will make a full end, as decreed, in the midst of all the earth. (Isaiah 10:20–23)

The works of the prophets were fundamental in the development of Judaism because they helped shape a new understanding of who God was. They also formed new views of the covenants of Abraham, Moses, and David. The prophets described the basic principle of Judaic monotheism—the denial of the existence of any other gods but Yahweh. Various prophets give details of Yahweh's character and his desires for humanity. Amos, the earliest of the Biblical prophets, claims that God is the one who controls history and nature. He states that Yahweh is a universal God who cares about the morals of all nations, not just Israel. Amos brings out the idea that Israel had a special responsibility to obey God's Law because Israel had the privilege of being chosen by God. These themes were developed by other prophets such as Isaiah, Jeremiah, Hosea, and Zephaniah. They

added the ideas that God is holy (that is, beyond human experience), mysterious, and utterly superior to human beings. On the other hand, they said that God is close to humanity because of His compassion and love for people.

The ideas of the prophets are often called "ethical monotheism." This means that their ideas focused on the parts of God's Law concerning what is right and wrong. The prophets looked at more than simply how to worship Yahweh. They concentrated on the part of the Law that stated that God wants justice. The prophets believed that humanity is basically sinful and offends God by breaking the spirit of the Law. One vision of the prophets is that there will be a future Day of Judgment. On that day, God will appear to judge the nation and individuals as well. God will separate the guilty from the innocent and dole out punishments and rewards. Exile from the Promised Land was seen as the penalty to be paid by a corrupt nation. To be counted among the righteous, individuals must seek God by obeying his commandments, doing what is morally right, and being humble.

Although they preached the Day of Judgment, the prophets also had hope that God's chosen people would be saved. Even though Israel might sin and be punished, God would keep his promise that Israel would always exist. God would save a "righteous remnant" and return it in peace and joy to the Promised Land. There, an ideal nation would live, full of people who knew God and practiced his justice. The new nation, with Jerusalem as its capital, would be the "beacon of light" for all the nations.

The prophets believed that the Messiah would rule the new kingdom as God's servant on earth. In keeping with the Davidic Covenant, the Messiah was to be from the House of David. Ideas about the character of the Messiah vary among the prophets. Depending on when the prophet existed, the Messiah was seen as militant or peaceful. Later prophets tended to think of the Messiah as a mediator between God and humanity, a teacher of justice and the Law, and the priestly or spiritual head of the new kingdom.

The prophets' ideas, therefore, changed the Yahwism of the nomadic and tribal people and the Yahwism of the Monarchy.

The ancient ideals were adapted and became larger principles that better fit a nation coexisting with other nations or a nation in exile. The work of the prophets certainly made it possible for the belief in Yahweh and his special relationship to Israel, to survive the destruction of Israel and Judah, and to flourish in later generations in very different circumstances.

The Exile

Biblical tradition presents the Exile as the second major experience for Israel. Unlike the Exodus, which was a joyful event, the Exile is presented as a period of punishment for the nation's sins. Return from exile happened only because God's people had passed a serious test of faith and God had forgiven them.

From the rather scanty sources available for the period of the Exile, it is known that the Babylonian king Nebuchadnezzar destroyed Jerusalem in 587 B.C.E. By 582 B.C.E., Nebuchadnezzar had exiled to southern Mesopotamia the political, religious, and intellectual leaders of Judah, along with a sizable portion of its population. The exiles lived in small communities near Babylon, where they were exposed to the most wealthy and powerful city of the ancient world. Jerusalem, even at its height, certainly seemed unsophisticated and poor when compared to Babylon. The Bible suggests that the exiles questioned Yahweh's power, especially when compared with the more visible power of the gods who ruled a nation as successful and favored as Babylon. They also questioned the status of the covenant between God and Israel.

The prophets' messages from the period of the Monarchy held the answers to some of the exiles' questions. In exile, the prophets continued the work of defining the new identity of Israel and God's expectations of his people. The prophet known as Second Isaiah stressed Israel's role as God's servant and foretold that God would save and forgive Israel. The prophet Ezekiel replaced political Israel, which had been destroyed, with a spiritual Israel. Ezekiel kept the idea of God and his promise apart from the life of the Temple and the other national institutions of Israel that had been destroyed. He stressed that the Jewish people should strictly follow the Law,

and he focused on their individual devotion to God. Because of this, Ezekiel is often called the Father of Judaism.

The community in exile developed its own identity. Its people carefully observed the Law, including the rules for the Sabbath, and they carried out formal religious practices. Communal prayer services, forerunners of the synagogue services, were held. Education of the people, especially the young, took on new importance. For the sake of education, the traditions and history of the Israelites were written down and collected in the works that would ultimately form parts of the Hebrew Bible.

CHAPTER 3

The Restoration to the Present

*J*udaism has the notable characteristic of holding on to its roots through thick and thin. Thus from Canaan to Egypt, in Egypt through the Exodus and into the Wilderness, during the Conquest of Canaan, through the Monarchy, and into the Exile, the early Jews were bound together by their basic beliefs. Rabbis and other Jewish leaders made this possible by continually adapting the religion to the changing conditions of the people.

The second period of Jewish history begins with the resettling of the Judahites in Judah. It extends to today, when Jews live and practice their faith all over the world. Its followers have dispersed and wandered, founded new communities and cultures, and met with enormous challenges. But by working together to find new ways to obey the Law under altered conditions, the Jews have preserved the foundations of their faith.

Restoration: The Persian Period

The Biblical books of Ezra and Nehemiah are our primary sources for information about the period of the Restoration. Knowledge of the Persian Empire and its policies, gathered from non-Biblical sources, also helps to shape our understanding of

this era. In 537 B.C.E., Cyrus, King of the Medes and Persians, conquered Babylon. It was general Persian policy that conquered peoples could govern their internal affairs so long as they accepted Persian rule regarding external matters, such as taxes paid to Persia and international relations. The Persians considered a group of people to be a nation capable of self-government if it had a body of law to govern its people. The exiled Judahites in Babylon certainly qualified. In 532 B.C.E., King Cyrus permitted the exiles to return to Jerusalem, in the land that they called Judah, and allowed them to govern themselves according to their own laws.

By all accounts, the exiles returned to a land that was far from the paradise envisioned by some of the prophets. Jerusalem was in ruins, enemies surrounded the new community, and the people experienced serious hardships. Hopes of restoring the Monarchy and total independence vanished. Despite their troubled times, the community focused on rebuilding the Temple; it was finished in 516 B.C.E. and is known in the history of Judaism as the Second Temple. The prophets Haggai and Zechariah figure prominently in this period as messengers of a new era to come, with its center at the Second Temple in Jerusalem.

Even though the Temple was completed, the community remained in very low spirits. Other rebuilding efforts proceeded slowly, and the community gradually relaxed its standards of obedience to the Law. According to the Hebrew Bible, two men had enormous influence in reshaping the struggling community and pointing it in a more positive direction. Nehemiah, a high official of the Persian King and a Jew, was authorized by the king to rebuild the walls of Jerusalem and attend to the problems the community faced. Ezra, a scribe sent from Babylon, instructed the people in the Law. Ezra adopted the Law to the new circumstances in a way that led to the community accepting it as its "constitution." As a result of these changes, Persia recognized Judah as a legal community.

By the fourth century B.C.E., Judah was prospering and its society was governed in every detail by the Law. Writing and editing of ancient texts had continued from the time of the Exile, and the Law of the Hebrew Bible took the same form as the

Torah of today. At the same time, the daily language of the community changed from the Hebrew language to Aramaic, the international language of the era.

Judah was not the only community of Jewish exiles. At the fall of Jerusalem in 587 B.C.E., a group that included the prophet Jeremiah had fled to Egypt and developed another thriving community. The community in Babylon, however, made up of people from the time of the Exile, became particularly wealthy and influential. Some of its members, such as Nehemiah, Esther, and Mordecai, achieved high status in the Persian court. In a sense, the beginnings of the Diaspora were in this Persian period. The former Israelites/Judahites became distinguished as a people, the people we call the Jews. Though they lived in communities where they could not participate in the religious traditions of the Temple, they did observe the Law. Thus no matter where they lived, the Jews were defined not by the national boundaries centering on Judah and Jerusalem but by their practice of Judaism.

The Hellenistic Period

Existing Jewish communities grew and prospered. New communities developed along the trade routes of the empire of Alexander the Great. The Greek word *diaspora* was used for the collection of these Jewish centers, many of which were far from Jerusalem. Alexander the Great, a famous general and king of Macedonia, conquered and ruled much of the ancient Near East between 336 and 323 B.C.E. Legend has it that Alexander the Great treated the Jews very well. However, Greek culture spread through the Near East in the times of Alexander and his successors, and this was a great threat to Judaism. First, the Jews of the Diaspora changed their language to Greek, which was the new international language. With the coming of the Greek language, Greek thought made inroads into traditional Jewish beliefs. Some Jews turned to the Greek philosophers for guidance. To meet the needs of Jews who no longer knew Hebrew, the Hebrew Bible was translated into Greek in the third century B.C.E. This text of the Bible is called the Septuagint.

When Alexander's generals divided his empire, Judah, by then called Judaea, fell to Egyptian rulers, the Ptolemies. Then

 *A Jewish family lighting the menorah during the celebration of Hanukkah.*

Seleucus, one of Alexander's ablest generals, seized it in 198 B.C.E. and established his own dynasty, the Seleucides. To counter threats of revolt in Judaea and Jerusalem, the Seleucid ruler, Antiochus (Epiphanes) IV, banned the practice of Judaism and attempted to force Hellenism, or Greek culture and religion, on the Jews. He prohibited observance of the Sabbath and circumcision (a religious ritual) under penalty of death. He burned

copies of the Law, and he raised an altar to the Greek god Zeus in the Temple. Torturing and executing those who refused to comply, he forced Jews to eat pork and make sacrifices to idols. His repeated acts of brutality and his efforts to destroy the Law finally sparked a revolt led by a devout Jewish family called the Maccabees. The Maccabees won independence for Judah, as recorded in the books of Maccabees (included in some Christian Bibles but not the Hebrew Bible). In 165 B.C.E., the Maccabees occupied Jerusalem and rebuilt and dedicated the altar for Yahweh at the Temple. The Hanukkah (Rededication) festival, also known as the Feast of Lights, celebrated by Jews today, commemorates this victory. The Maccabean revolt centered on a rekindling of faith based on the observance of the Law. From this period came the Biblical book of Daniel, with its message of reassurance to the faithful and visions of the new era to come.

The Maccabees, also known as the Hasmonaean Dynasty, restored Judaea's independence and established its religious freedom. The new nation of Judaea was ruled by the High Priest. Under the new dynasty, the Jews were fiercely anti-Hellenistic but became involved in the political intrigues of the age, which ultimately involved the emerging power of Rome. They were also divided into groups with widely differing political and religious views. The most famous of these were the Sadducees and Pharisees.

The Sadducees and Pharisees vied with one another. The Sadducees were members of a priestly family who believed in the religious authority of the Torah, or the first five books of the Bible alone. They opposed the more progressive Pharisees, or "separatists," who helped develop an elaborate system of oral laws used to apply the written laws of Moses or the Torah to Jewish life. The Sanhedrin, or the highest governing council of the Jews until the Fall of Jerusalem in 70 C.E., was established as the central authority for all legal decisions and settled the more complex cases of law and the debates between the Sadducees and Pharisees.

The Essenes were another well-known group in Judea. They were a group of ascetics, very self-disciplined people, numbering about 4,000, who led a communal life that aimed at

avoiding contamination by worldly impurity. In the late 1940s and the 1950s, the remains of an Essene monastery and several jars of ancient scrolls were found at Qumran near the Dead Sea in Jordan. These writings, known as the Dead Sea Scrolls, the oldest Biblical manuscripts yet found, seem to belong to a group of Essenes.

The Roman Period

By the first century B.C.E., Rome had entered the international scene. The Jews in Israel were suffering from internal strife, and the state was weak and ripe for Roman interference. By 47 B.C.E., Israel was called Judaea and was subject to Roman rule. Rome ruled much as Persia had done. A Roman governor oversaw Roman interests in Judaea but left the governing of internal matters to the Sanhedrin and the Herodean kings, a Jewish dynasty reigning in Judaea.

Judaism itself underwent a major upset with the birth of Christianity, the religion founded by Jesus. Early converts to Christianity were Jews in Judaea. Then many of the Greek Jews of the Diaspora took up the new religion. Some Jewish authorities considered these Judaeo-Christians to be heretics, or antibelievers. Others saw the new faith as a sect of Judaism. Christianity rapidly converted many pagans who did not know the Jewish foundations of the new religion and concentrated only on Jesus' teachings. As the Law of Moses lost importance in the eyes of many early Christians, the Jewish authorities responded by tightening up the observance of the Law for faithful Jews.

The Herodean kings of Judaea sought the approval of Rome. Under them, Judaea dissolved after a series of Jewish rebellions and religious conflicts. The most famous revolt was against Roman rule. It was led by the Zealots, a militant Jewish sect. In 68 C.E., the Romans suppressed the revolt. The last stronghold of the Zealots was Masada, a fortress built on a huge rock near the Dead Sea. The historian Josephus described the Roman siege of Masada: In the end, the Zealots chose to kill themselves rather than be taken by the Romans. In 70 C.E., Emperor Titus destroyed the Second Temple, demolished

Jerusalem, and disbanded the Sanhedrin. Judaea continued to exist only as a province of Rome. In 130 C.E., the Emperor Hadrian rebuilt Jerusalem as the pagan city Aelia Capitolina. The resulting Bar Cochba Revolt (132–135 C.E.) left half a million Jews dead. The name of Judaea was then changed to Syria-Palestina, and Jews were forbidden to enter the now pagan city of Jerusalem under penalty of death.

The Jews were persecuted throughout the Roman Empire. The Christians also thought that the destruction of Jerusalem and the defeat of the Jews was evidence that God had abandoned them and transferred his favor to the Christians. When the cruel treatment of Christians was banned by the Edict of Milan in 313 C.E. and the Christian religion became acceptable in the Roman Empire in 325 C.E., the Jews were still suffering persecution at the hands of the Romans.

The events connected with the destruction of the Second Temple, and the period following, were in some ways like the events in the period of the Babylonian Exile. The Jews' response to this exile in the Roman Period was similar to that of the Babylonian and Persian periods. In the six centuries following the destruction of the Temple, the Jews of Judaea and the Diaspora withdrew again into their Diaspora communities. They concentrated on building a way of life through which they could preserve their identity as Jews. The religion that emerged from this period, sometimes called rabbinic Judaism, was the form of Judaism from which all modern branches of the Jewish religion descend. It was shaped by a group of rabbis (literally, "my great ones," "masters," or "teachers") whose diligent study and writings span the era from 70 C.E. to the Islamic conquest of the Near East in 640 C.E.

Rabbinic Judaism drew on the heritage of the past, the practice of the Law, and the Messianic hope for the future. While the hope for the coming of the Messiah was always strong, the new age that he would introduce seemed far in the future. In fact, it was only gradually during the rabbinical era that questions about the Messianic age—and its character—arose among Jews. By this time, the Jews had the Hebrew Bible to serve as a guide and written source for the history that had gone before them. In

the area of the Law, however, there was need for continued interpretation and clarification if the communities were to achieve the devoted and obedient lives they believed God demanded of them in their continually new circumstances.

The rabbis accepted the Hebrew Bible as the authoritative written source of knowledge about God and the Law, given by God to Moses at Mount Sinai. At the same time, they also believed that Moses received an oral, or spoken, tradition of knowledge. The oral tradition gave more details about the written tradition of the Hebrew Bible and how it must be adapted to new circumstances. The rabbis believed that this tradition was passed on from Moses to Joshua, to the other great leaders of the past, to the prophets, to their ancestors, and finally, to the rabbis.

The rabbis, learned and pious men, set about writing down the oral tradition so that the Jews might better understand what was expected of them as they prepared for the coming of the Messiah. The first of the rabbis' writings is called the Mishnah. The Mishnah dates from about 200 C.E. and is a collection of interpretations of the Law based on the oral tradition. To extend this fairly brief text, rabbis in Palestine and Babylonia produced a series of commentaries on the Mishnah. These writings are known as the Gemara. The Gemara is a more complex document, since it is not a simple explanation of the Mishnah, but records the debates and disagreements of the various Mishnah interpreters. The Gemara is thus less authoritative than the Torah and Mishnah, since it provides the opinions and interpretations of scholars rather than the written (Torah) or oral (Mishnah) law itself. All three elements (Torah, Mishnah, and Gemara) make up the Talmud, but only the first two (Torah and Mishnah) have the full power of law. The Jerusalem Talmud dates from about 400 C.E. The Babylonian Talmud, which had more influence on the Jews through the ages, was written in about 500 C.E. Yet another text, the Midrash, is a collection of sermons and other explanations of the Bible. It was compiled between 300 and 600 C.E. The Torah, the rest of the Hebrew Bible, the Mishnah, the Talmud, and the Midrash became the basic written sources for all subsequent rabbinic Judaism. To this day, these works provide the authoritative sources of guidance for the Jews.

From Rabbinic Judaism to Modern Times
(640 to 1492)

Because Jews lived in many countries with different customs and social orders, the rabbinic way of life took on many variations. However, a certain type of uniting also took place within Judaism when the religion and rule of Islam, founded by Muhammad, came to dominate the Middle East and North Africa. This happened in the seventh century. In the middle of the eighth century, the capital of Muslim (Islamic) rule moved from Syria to Baghdad. Baghdad then became the center of power and legal activity, not only for the Muslims but also for the Jews. The Babylonian Talmud guided the lives of Jews in this region and in areas under its influence. As Jews established new communities, they spread the influence of the Babylonian Talmud to all the Jews who lived under Muslim political authority. So despite the variations of countries, customs, and social orders, rabbinic Judaism grew as a unifying force for the Jewish people of this vast region.

The *yeshiva*, an academy or center of legal learning, played the most important role in unifying Judaism. Before the Muslim dominance, there had been three *yeshivot* (academies)—one in Palestine and two in Babylonia—where the Palestinian and Babylonian Talmuds had been written. The yeshiva was a center of religious power, so when Muslim power was centered in Baghdad, the religious power in Judaism was centered in the yeshivot there. The heads of the yeshivot developed new ways of unifying Judaism through writing and distributing legal literature. The first procedure that unified Judaism was a system called the *teshuvah*, a response to a legal question. At the different centers of Judaism throughout the Muslim-dominated world, the teshuvah helped the Jews to interpret the Law. In the many Jewish communities, the responses in the teshuvah were read aloud in the synagogues. This gave them and their source in Baghdad a strong religious and legal authority. The *taqqanah*, or legal ordinance, was another procedure or means of strengthening this authority. These new laws, or changes to existing laws, made the Talmud fit new circumstances of living.

The heads of the Babylonian yeshivot in Baghdad also wrote commentaries on the Mishnah and the Talmud. In these commentaries, they often traced their knowledge and wisdom back to Yahweh and the time of Moses. By pointing out that their source was divine, they gained more respect and authority. The heads of these yeshivot further strengthened their religious and legal influence by training and giving official licenses to judges. They also ran training sessions for the study of law. The people who took these sessions gained respect and authority because their skills in religious law came from and grew from the highest rabbinic authority. By the beginning of the eleventh century, they had brought a unifying religious and social form of legal procedure to all the centers of Judaism throughout the Middle East and North Africa.

One of the main centers of Jewish culture during this period was at Kairouan, the capital of what is now the North African country of Tunisia. A house of Jewish legal study was in place in Kairouan by the end of the ninth century. It was an academy in the tradition of the Babylonian Talmud. Then in the tenth century, it began to show the influences of its most famous leader, Hushi'el. He seems to have come from Italy, where the influence of the Palestinian Talmud was very strong. Another center of the Babylonian Talmud, led by Isaac Alfasi, developed during the tenth and eleventh centuries at Fez, in present-day Morocco.

In tenth-century Egypt, there was an independent center of Jewish life. However, this community soon felt the influence of the Palestinian Talmudic tradition, then that of the Babylonian Talmud. Cairo, Egypt, became an even more important center of Jewish scholarship when Moses Maimonides arrived there about 1165. He was such a powerful Jewish legal scholar that he was able to substitute his own code of Jewish law, the Mishneh Torah (renewal of the Law), for the Babylonian Talmud as the centerpiece of Jewish legal education. Maimonides' influence spread into Yemen, despite the long history of loyalty in this center of Judaism to the *gaon*, or religious and legal leader, of Babylonia. Eventually, the Mishneh Torah became the ruling code of Jewish Law in Yemen. The many commentaries on Maimonides' books, including the Mishneh Torah, support the point that Maimonides had a strong sway in this region.

Maimonides' influence shows a break with the Babylonian Talmudic tradition. The Jewish Karaites took this break even further. The Karaite revolt took place in Iran in the eighth century. Its leader was Anan ben David, who created communities of antirabbinic Jews. The principle, "Search thoroughly into the Torah and do not depend upon any opinion," is attributed to him. In fact, the Karaites totally rejected the oral Torah and asked for reliance on the Bible alone. In a sense, the Karaites forged a complete revolt against rabbinic Judaism. Karaism seems to have come from an outcry against Baghdad as the center of both Islamic and Jewish influences. In Judaism, Karaism took (and in its present-day form takes) the character of an antirabbinic movement. This reliance on the written Torah alone grew into a strong alternative to rabbinic Judaism by the tenth century. It reached its apex of influence in the eleventh and twelfth centuries in Iran.

Judaism was not limited to the Middle East and North Africa. From the many ancient synagogues in Greece and Rome we know that Judaism was found in Southern Europe as early as the first and second centuries. When Iberia (Portugal and Spain) was conquered by Islam in the early eighth century, this opened up a world of new migration for the Jewish people. By the tenth century, Iberia's Jewish population numbered 250,000.

For the most part, the Jews of Iberia followed the religious and legal codes of Babylonian Jewry. This community's Judaism, called Sefardic (the Hebrew word for "Iberian") Judaism, was strongly influenced by both Alfasi of Fez in the late eleventh century and Moses Maimonides before his departure for Egypt about 1165. Both men brought a strong philosophical tone to Spanish-Portuguese Judaism and stimulated one of the golden periods of philosophy in Judaic history. Maimonides' *Guide for the Perplexed* is the greatest Jewish philosophical work of this classical era. Other works that share this thoughtful tone of Judaism include the eleventh century writings of Ibn Gabirol, twelfth century Biblical commentaries of Mosheh ibn 'Ezra', and the philosophical works of Levi ben Gershom (1288–1344) and Hasdai Crescas (1410). This philosophical tendency of the Sefardic Jewish world was supported by developments in

Jewish mysticism called the *cabala*. Scholars of the cabala studied the mysteries, or hidden truths, of the Torah. The more traditional Jews of France and Italy opposed the philosophical drive of the Sefardic Jews.

In the early ninth century, the Emperor Charlemagne ruled most of what is now Central and Western Europe. His economic policies at that time encouraged Jewish merchants to do business in his French Empire and later in the German Empire. Cut off from the large and tightly knit communities elsewhere, these Jewish communities needed to forge a new way. Their new *Ashkenazic*, or Germanic, form of Judaism was decisively influenced by two great forces of the twelfth century. The first was the movement of the *Hasidim*, or pietists, who began as a small group of religious Jews who were ascetics (upholding the highest religious and moral standards). Their influence grew beyond their own narrow circle. Eventually, theirs became the central form of Jewish piety in Germany and Western Europe. The second force in the development of Ashkenazic Judaism was the commentary made on the Bible and the Babylonian Talmud by the late eleventh century rabbinic master Rashi. In his commentary, Rashi tried to relate the Talmudic traditions of the Mediterranean world to the practices of Jews living in the world of Latin Christians. His was a more complex form of law. This new form of law, along with the ascetic practices of the Hasidim, changed Sefardic Judaism into Ashkenazic Judaism. Ashkenazic Judaism developed a tradition of its own, including its own Germanic language, Yiddish.

Ashkenazic Judaism, however, did not develop smoothly. From the eleventh to the thirteenth centuries, the Christian Crusades were undertaken to rid the Holy Land of Muslims. In practical terms, many of the crusaders, as they reviewed their efforts to cleanse the Holy Land, judged that they might best begin at home and cleanse their immediate world of the infidel Jews. To them, no more convincing reason could be found to explain the natural disaster of the Black Death of 1349 than that it was caused by the Jews. Popular Christian imagination began to blame the Jews for this catastrophe, accusing them of poisoning the wells of Europe. As the Jews became the objects of such

hatred, they were expelled from northern France and Germany and migrated eastward to Bohemia, Moravia, Hungary, Poland, and Lithuania. In all these regions, Ashkenazic Judaism toughened from the sobering realities of long persecution.

A number of other, far-flung Jewish communities also developed during this period. A community of black Jews in Ethiopia called *Falashas* ("exiles" or "wanderers") strengthened their numbers in the early sixth century with an influx of Jews from southern Arabia. The Falashas trace their roots back to a time before the fourth century. Some documents dating from 718 also show the presence of a community of Jews in Chinese Turkistan. The first synagogue in K'ai-feng, the capital of Honan Province, dates from 1163. During the tenth century, there were Jews in Bukhara and Samark and in the southern part of what would become the

■ *A cantor sounds the shofar, or ram's horn, at the end of the Day of Atonement in the synagogue of Cochin, India.*

Soviet Union. Jews in Cochin, India, have copper tablets from about 1000, showing that Jews at the time were given certain lands and privileges in that region. So even though most of the Jews were in the Middle East, North Africa, and in the Sefardic and Ashkenazic regions, independent clusters were found in other localities throughout the world.

From 1492 to the Enlightenment (1789)

The year 1492 was the official date for the expulsion of the Jews from Spain. That exodus, however, began with certain pressures in 1391. Continued violence against Sefardic Jews offered them three alternatives: convert to Christianity, suffer martyrdom by dying rather than denying their religion, or flee. The same alternatives had been given to Jews in France in 1306 and 1394 and to the Jews in Portugal in 1497. During those trying times, a number of Jews were forced to convert to Christianity, but they carried on their Jewish practices. They were called *Marranos*. It was often difficult for Christian authorities to determine whether or not the conversions to Christianity were authentic. Part of the mission of the Spanish Inquisition from 1478 to 1492 was to make this determination. These examinations led at times to the persecution of the Marranos, who either fled to southern France where they pretended not to be Jews, or to Turkey where they pretended not to be Christians, or to Italy where they could choose either option, or to tolerant Amsterdam, as did the family of the philosopher Baruch Spinoza. The Sefardic Jews who did not convert and who chose to flee moved for the most part back to the Muslim world.

Muhammad, the founder of Islam, had guaranteed protection for the Jews because they also were "people of the book." But this guarantee held the condition that the Jews live as lower-class citizens in Muslim lands. In effect, this meant that their houses of worship could not stand out, that they wore garments that distinguished them from other citizens, and that they pay special taxes. In 1391, under these conditions, Sefardic Jews began a mass emigration to Algeria. There they met native communities of Jews that had been there for centuries. Because of their superior education, their vast numbers, and their cultural

self-esteem, the Sefardic Jews took over the leadership positions in Algerian Judaism. In 1492, when more than 150,000 Jews left Spain, most went to Morocco. These Sefardic Jews quickly took control of the less vibrant Judaism of native Jewish Moroccans.

Yet even before 1492, word had spread among Jews that Turkey would welcome them. To avoid persecution where they were, they migrated in droves. They brought with them their attachments from the regions they had left. In fact, at that time in Istanbul and Salonika, Turkey, there were more than forty different, and indeed separate, congregations of Jews who were anchored in the traditions of their individual origins.

In sixteenth-century Turkey, a great revival of Jewish culture was dominated and unified by Sefardic influences. The language of this community was that of the dominant Sefardic Jews, Ladino (Castilian Spanish, with a mixture of Hebrew, Turkish, and Slavic words). Not all Jews under Islamic rule shared in the resurgence of Judaism in Turkey. The Jews who moved to Persia were subjected to especially harsh, discriminatory laws. Even the successes of Turkey were not long lasting, for the eighteenth century found the Jews of the Arab and Turkish lands to be poor, vulnerable, humiliated, and insecure.

The Sefardic Jews who fled to Christian lands that were tolerant, such as Italy, found Jewish communities with traditions that had already been strengthened by the Ashkenazic Jews who had arrived a century before. Italy became a melting pot of different forms of Judaism, with each new Sefardic community preserving its traditions: Castilian, Barcelonian, Catalonian, and Provençal. Rome in the sixteenth century had nine synagogues, each anchored in a different tradition. This toleration was not long-lived. In 1553, many copies of the Talmud were burned, and in 1555, the city-states created ghettos to which all Jews were herded for identification and control.

Sefardic Jews also fled to South America, but persecution followed them to lands under the dominion of Spain and Portugal. When Recife, Brazil, was captured by the Dutch, it became a haven for Jews. Yet the Dutch held power only from 1630 to 1654. When the Portuguese recaptured the city, the Jews fled back to Holland, to the West Indies where earlier Jewish

communities resided, or to New Amsterdam (New York). Sefardic Judaism dominated small communities of Jews in the United States until massive new immigrations of Ashkenazic Jews began much later in 1881. The Sefardic Jews of this earlier period were much better educated and generally more sophisticated than the Ashkenazic Jews.

The Ashkenazic Jews, driven out of many cities in Germany, Bohemia, and Moravia, looked eastward toward Poland. Commercial growth and religious toleration also encouraged them to migrate to Poland and Lithuania. Commerce and artisanry became the chief occupations for Jews in this region, and their numbers had swelled by the middle of the seventeenth century to about 350,000. They enjoyed a strong legal autonomy under the control of the Polish kings. Yet their lives there in the sixteenth and seventeenth centuries were not without serious problems. The Catholic Church, as part of its Counter-Reformation, expelled many Jews from Polish cities in the late sixteenth century. A Cossack uprising in the Ukraine in the middle of the seventeenth century killed a vast number of Ukrainian Jews before driving out all the others.

Jews in all parts of the Christian and Muslim world lived through a very difficult period from 1492, when they were formally driven from Spain, until the Enlightenment in the eighteenth century. They did have great success in building communities, especially in the sixteenth century in Algeria, Morocco, Turkey, and in Italy and Poland. But throughout the world, their trials and troubles grew in the seventeenth and eighteenth centuries. It is no wonder that the Enlightenment in Europe with its call for emancipation brought new hope to the Jewish people.

From the Age of Emancipation to World War I (1789 to 1914)

The start of the French Revolution is a symbolic year in the history of modern Judaism. It was not only the end of an old regime that had brought much suffering; it was also the beginning of regimes with new possibilities for the Jewish people. Modern states, such as France, Germany, and England, were

becoming secularized, or religiously neutral. Toleration was the wave of the day. Great Jewish thinkers, like the philosopher Moses Mendelssohn (1729–1786), believed that Judaism in such a secular atmosphere could thrive better than Christianity.

This hope was not always fulfilled in the way Mendelssohn and others had envisioned. In Muslim lands, for instance, the emancipation brought modern, secular ideas, and technical skills. This was unwittingly occasioned by efforts of modern European Jews who wanted to help poor and uneducated Jews outside of Europe. Yet Muslim lands resisted any European intrusion. Because this new training came from Europe, all Jews became identified as foreigners and never were welcomed into full participation in the Muslim societies. Therefore, most Jewish communities in Algeria, Morocco, and other Islamic territories disappeared or became very small.

The French occupations of Italy in 1796–1798 and 1800–1815 brought emancipation to Jews within some Italian city-states. These occupations had the strong effect of opening up educational opportunities and stimulating scholarship that, among other things, traced the history of Jewish sources and practices of worship. However, the nonreligious tendency in these Enlightenment movements at times led to the corruption of Jewish community life and the abandonment of religious observances as more Jews became assimilated into secular culture.

In the Germanic world, after the French Revolution, Jews tended to split into two staunchly different groups. One was the more Westernized and secularized elite; the other was the Yiddish-speaking, more traditional religious population. In Germany and Austria, those who advanced in society abandoned Yiddish for German and rejected much of the Judaism that was traditional and viewed as uncultured. Reform and Neo-Orthodox forms of Judaism were developed that reduced the importance of national characteristics and underscored the more universal values within Judaism that all men could respect. These forms of the religion would allow for greater acceptance and assimilation into the broader secular society. Yet in the Austrian section of Galicia and in Poland, Lithuania, Russia, and Hungary, strong elements of traditional Judaism remained, especially

among the poorer and more simple Jews of the villages and towns. Mosheh Sofer (1762–1839) even led a movement to restore tradition, claiming that "Everything new is forbidden by the Torah."

The small group of Jews that had come from Recife, Brazil, to New Amsterdam had increased their numbers through modest immigration and had formed other Jewish communities in Newport (Rhode Island), Philadelphia, Charleston, Savannah, Baltimore, Richmond, and Boston. Some even went westward toward Cincinnati, St. Louis, and New Orleans. Gradually, they became Americanized, and by 1885, most Jews in America belonged to Reform congregations. In 1881, however, waves of Jewish immigrants, mostly the hard-working, poor, and uneducated from Austria, Poland, Lithuania, Russia, and Hungary, began entering the United States and Canada. By the eve of World War I, slightly more than thirty years later, 1,175,000 Jewish refugees had arrived and brought with them their Orthodox beliefs and practices. The split in Jewry, evident in Germanic lands, between Reform and Orthodox Jews, was newly evident in the New World. The Orthodox Jews became the vast majority; in numbers, the Reform Jews were a fringe minority of the successful, well-educated, and sophisticated. The history of the Jewish people in America from 1881, until the beginning of World War I was the story of a people attempting to find a new identity while holding on to their religious traditions. The achievement of this new identity was based on a variety of ways of envisioning their "Jewishness."

From World War I to the Present

Shortly after World War I, the United States government passed legislation that limited the annual quotas (numbers of persons allowed to enter), restricting the number of immigrants to the country. Jews at that time were fleeing the anti-Semitism (anti-Jewish feeling) that was growing in Germany. The lower United States quotas forced these Jews to look to South America, Canada, or elsewhere for refuge. The most dominant event of this period, however, was the Holocaust: the intentional destruction of European Jewry by the dictator of Germany, Adolf Hitler,

and his Nazi war machine as it marched through Europe in World War II. The individual horror behind the grim statistics of the murders of 6,000,000 Jews in concentration camps was portrayed in *The Diary of Anne Frank*, written by a young Dutch girl who was discovered in hiding with her family in Amsterdam and then killed by the Nazis. The writings of Elie Wiesel, Primo Levi, and many others relate the personal experiences of the authors during the Holocaust. In *Night*, Wiesel tells of his first night in a Nazi death camp:

> *Never shall I forget that night, the first night in camp, which has turned my life into one long night, seven times cursed and seven times sealed. Never shall I forget that smoke. Never shall I forget the little faces of the children, whose bodies I saw turned into wreaths of smoke beneath a silent blue sky.*

■ *Prisoners, young and old, leave the Buchenwald concentration camp to receive treatment at an American hospital.*

Jewish Losses During World War II	
Poland	2,850,000
U.S.S.R.	1,500,000
Rumania	425,000
Czechoslovakia	240,000
Hungary	200,000
Lithuania	130,000
Germany	110,000
Holland	105,000
France	90,000
Latvia	80,000
Greece	60,000
Yugoslavia	55,000
Austria	45,000
Belgium	40,000
Italy	15,000
Bulgaria	7,000
Denmark, Norway, Luxembourg, Estonia	5,000
Total:	5,957,000

These children's vile deaths and the deaths of their elders shook the Jewish and non-Jewish world alike. Even the growing anti-Semitism rampant in Germany after World War I, as German citizens tried to find scapegoats for their defeat, could not come close to predicting this horror. Nor could the anti-Semitism in Poland, demanding strong nationalism and exclusion of non-Christians, prepare the imagination of the world for such cruelty.

The aftermath of the Holocaust left Jews around the world in shock and in revolt. European Jewry was almost completely destroyed. Many of the surviving Jews sought a safe place to reclaim their lives. The main European options for resettlement were in England and France. For many, the most appealing options were the newborn state of Israel and the United States. As nationalism in postwar Arab countries developed, many Jews left those lands. Algerian Jews headed to a welcoming France. Moroccan Jews who had not fled at an earlier time opted for Israel. Less than 10 percent of the Jewish population who lived in Muslim countries at the end of the war remain in those countries today. Small communities still exist in Morocco, Iran, and Turkey, but more than a million Jews have fled Arab lands for Israel and the West since 1948.

Italian Jewry has bounced back somewhat from the experiences of World War II. This is especially true in larger cities like Rome and Milan. In Spain, Jews were promised equal rights in 1966. Some 10,000 Jews, mostly Sefardic, have since settled there. A small community of less than 1,000 Jews has also settled in Portugal.

Over all, the two strongest centers of Jewish life during this period of resettlement have been the United States and the state of Israel. The United States drew vast numbers of immigrants between 1881 and World War I. This slowed to a trickle because of the stringent immigration laws of 1921 and 1924, and many Jews headed to Canada and to Central and South America. However, after World War II, the American Jewish community grew in strength, prestige, and influence within American society. The events of the Holocaust fostered a heightened sense of Jewishness in the American communities, from which emerged

a strong fundraising body for rescue activities and an enormous growth in Jewish religious institutions.

The state of Israel began as a project of Zionism, the movement to reestablish a Jewish state in Palestine. The movement began in Eastern Europe in the nineteenth century and gained stature and international recognition through the work of Theodor Herzl (1860–1904) and Asher Ginsberg (1856–1927). Herzl and Ginsberg each had different ideas for what the movement should be. For Herzl, such a homeland would remove Jews from nations where anti-Semitism was strong and would give Jews a better chance of achieving economic success. Ginsberg stressed the cultural benefits of such a homeland: Jews there

■ *A celebration by a kibbutz family. Malka Ram, a founding member of the Degania Kibbutz, rejoices with four generations of her family.*

could live with Western values without having their Jewish identities obscured. Their efforts were not strongly applauded by most religious Jews, who saw the plan as a push for a secularist, or nonreligious, Jewish state.

Despite the opinions against it, the dream of the Zionists did come to fruition in the aftermath of the Holocaust. With the world community reeling from the barbarity of the Holocaust, world opinion began to favor more and more a place where Jews, violently ousted from their homes and homelands, could find their own identity. The opportunity to put this Zionist dream into practice came in 1948 with the founding of the State of Israel. It is to Israel that many Jews throughout the world—from Russia, Morocco, Ethiopia, Iraq, the surviving communities of Europe, indeed, from the world over—gathered to attempt a new form of Jewish living. Some came to work on cooperative farms, *kibbutzim*. Others joined in the development of healthy industry. All contributed to making Israel a strong, modern, democratic nation.

In a religious context, a distinction can be made between the State of Israel and Judaism as a religion. In fact, while 80 percent of the population of Israel are Jews, 15 percent are Muslim, and about 2 percent are Christian. The majority of Israel's Jews would not call themselves strongly religious. Statistically, less than 25 percent of them consider themselves Orthodox Jews. Many more, though, follow the tenets and practices of Judaism to varying degrees. Throughout their history, the Jews have felt a continuous link to Palestine, not only as the land of their ancestors, but also as the land promised by God to the children of Abraham, the children of the divine covenant. Even in modern times, a strong element of the faith and tradition of Israeli Jews is a return to their ancient homeland from the lands of exile or dispersal.

In a political context, the State of Israel is faced with enormous challenges. Israel is a political island in an Arab world. Though it is located on the eastern shore of the Mediterranean Sea, it is otherwise surrounded by the Arab countries of Egypt, Jordan, Syria, and Lebanon. Part of its territory is claimed by Arab Palestinians who also occupied much of the land of

Palestine before the mandate (an order to establish a government) for Palestine was given to Britain by the League of Nations in 1922. The United Nations tried to settle the conflict between British authorities, Jewish settlers, and Arab Palestinians by calling for separate Jewish and Arab states in 1947. The State of Israel was established the next year. Yet, battles have ensued with Arab neighbors ever since, and political stability has been continually challenged to the present day.

CHAPTER **4**

The Hebrew Bible:
An Overview

In the Islamic world, Muslims, Christians, and Jews are considered "people of the book." The book, of course, is the Bible. For the Jews, the Bible is the Hebrew Bible. The Christian Old Testament is the Hebrew Bible with a reordering of some of the texts and some additions. It is the one book that all three religions have in common, even if the ways in which each tradition reads the book might differ.

How did the Hebrew Bible come to be one book? The traditions of the Hebrew people were at first passed down by word of mouth. They were not written down. The stories of Abraham, of Moses, of prophets like Isaiah and Jeremiah were handed down through recitation of the important events of their lives. Most scholars now think that some of these traditions began to take on written form around 950 B.C.E.

The need to write the story must have become evident as the twelve tribes of Israel unified under the Monarchy. The various oral histories of the twelve tribes needed a unification that matched their new political unity. Later, with the split of the Monarchy into two kingdoms, another written account of the various aspects of Jewish history began to take shape in the

Northern Kingdom. After the fall of the Northern Kingdom to Assyria in 721 B.C.E., the people of the Northern Kingdom dispersed and began to marry outside their community. They lost contact with their story, abandoned their Jewish traditions, and disappeared as a community. Around the year 630 B.C.E., the people of the Southern Kingdom, led mainly by Josiah, began a reform based on the finding of a copy of "the book of the Torah," believed to have been the Biblical Book of Deuteronomy. More than ever, the people of the Southern Kingdom saw the importance of a more definitive written account of their story as a people and a strong commitment to their covenant with God. This alone, they believed, would save the Southern Kingdom from the fate suffered by the people of the Northern Kingdom. Josiah's reform and the recommitment of the Jewish people to their covenant with God kept the people of Judah centered as a community and brought them strength and unity even during the Babylonian Exile of 573–521 B.C.E. The Judahites' return to their homeland and their rebuilding of the Temple enabled them to reflect on their history in a new way, producing a fourth written tradition, more centered in the Temple and the worship owed to God. Thus there were, according to scholars who see the Hebrew Bible developing in this way, four different written traditions. Each version represented the story of the Jewish people at different times and in different circumstances. All four of these written versions of their history were pulled together around 400 B.C.E. and unified into the Hebrew Bible.

The Bible as God's Revelation

Jewish tradition accepts the Hebrew Bible as the disclosure, or revelation, of God's will, communicated over a long period of time to inspired individuals known as prophets. For the Jews, the story contained in these sacred Scriptures is not just an account of the trials of a people and their wars, their wanderings, their exiles and enslavements. It is a sacred story in which the ultimate meaning of life is revealed. It is also a story in which God is the main actor and director.

Perhaps the best way of showing how this perspective of Jewish faith brings a new level of meaning to life might be

through the story of Joseph, one of the twelve sons of Jacob. The other sons of Jacob became jealous of their brother and sold him into slavery. Joseph ended up in Egypt—first as a slave, but eventually as chief minister to Pharaoh. During a famine in their country, Joseph's brothers traveled to Egypt to find food, and Joseph gave them grain. Here is the way the story is told in the last chapter of Genesis:

> When Joseph's brothers saw that their father was dead, they said, "It may be that Joseph will hate us and pay us back for all the evil which we did to him." So they sent a message to Joseph, saying, "Your father gave us a command before he died, saying, 'Say to Joseph, Forgive I pray you, the transgression of your brothers and their sin, because they did evil to you. 'And now, we pray you, forgive the transgression of the servants of the God of your father." Joseph wept when they spoke to him. His brothers also came and fell down before him and said, "Behold we are your servants." But Joseph said to them, "Fear not, for am I in the place of God? As for you, you meant evil against me; but God meant it for good, to bring it about that many people should be kept alive, as they are today." (Genesis 50:15–20)

For Jewish believers, "human" events and intentions are not just human, and they cannot be explained in purely human terms. Indeed, the Jewish story and the stories of all their neighboring nations are, for the faithful Jew, God's story. The Hebrew Bible recounts a sacred story about God and his covenant, or agreement, with a particular people, the descendants of Abraham. It is also a story about their neighbors and God's plan for them in Israel's life. And likewise it is a story of the world they inhabit, created by God and ruled by Him. All nature and all history offers, for the believing Jew, a realm that one can only begin to understand when one sees it as a sacred world and a sacred history. Reading the Hebrew story leads the believer to see all the events in his or her own life and community in a different light, a sacred one. It is a story of the relationship between God and men.

The Books Recounting the Sacred Story

The Hebrew Bible contains twenty-four books and is traditionally divided into three sections: The Law (*Torah*); the Prophets (*Nebiyim*); and the Writings (*Ketubiyim*). If one takes the first letters of the three Hebrew words and adds the vowel *a* between them, one discovers the word that the Jews use to describe their Bible—*Tanak*. The three sections of the Tanak contain the sacred writings of the Jews:

■ *An ornamental cabinet containing the Torah scrolls in a synagogue in Kerala, India.*

The Law (*Torah*) consists of five books: Genesis, Exodus, Leviticus, Numbers, and Deuteronomy. The Law is also called the *Pentateuch*, which literally means "five scrolls or volumes." These first five books of the Bible were originally written on five scrolls of approximately equal length.

The Prophets (*Nebiyim*) consists of eight books divided into (a) Early Prophets: Joshua, Judges, (I and II) Samuel, and (I and II) Kings; and (b) Later Prophets: Isaiah, Jeremiah, Ezekiel, and The Twelve (which contains the teachings of the twelve minor prophets: Hosea, Joel, Amos, Obadiah, Jonah, Micah, Naham, Habakkuk, Zephaniah, Haggai, Zechariah, and Malachi).

The Writings (*Ketubiyim*) consists of eleven books: Psalms, Job, Proverbs, Ruth, Song of Songs, Ecclesiastes, Lamentations, Esther, Daniel, Ezra-Nehemiah, and Chronicles.

The Law (*Torah*)

The word *Torah* can have many different meanings. It can mean the first five books of the Hebrew Bible (Genesis, Exodus, Leviticus, Numbers, and Deuteronomy); it can mean the whole of the sacred writings that the Jewish people call *Tanak;* or it can be extended to include both the written Law and the whole tradition of interpretation of the Law handed down by the rabbis. Fundamentalist sects, such as the Samaritans and the Karaites, deny the oral tradition and would thus not admit it as Torah. For Samaritans, the Pentateuch alone is Torah; for Karaites, the whole written Bible is Torah.

Speaking of it in this first sense, the Torah, or Pentateuch, is the most important of the three sections of the Hebrew Bible. Genesis 1–11 presents God as the creator and ruler of the world and establishes his relationship with humanity. Genesis 12–50 speaks of how God chose Abraham to be father of the Hebrews and indicates the promises God made to him. Exodus tells of the escape from Egypt, the Covenant of Sinai, the Ten Commandments, and the Mosaic Code of Law. The remaining books (Leviticus, Numbers, and Deuteronomy) are concerned with the wilderness experience and the law. The Torah introduces the ideas of promise, choice, covenant, and law that run through the entire Hebrew Bible and which are the foundations of Judaism.

Thus the first five books of the Bible present the great themes of the Hebrew tradition: the promises made to Abraham and his descendants; the deliverance of Israel from the slavery of Egypt; the giving of the Law at Mount Sinai; God's guidance as the Hebrews wandered in the desert; the inheritance of the Promised Land. The Torah also introduces us to two of the great figures of the Hebrew Bible, Abraham and Moses, and to its greatest and central figure, God.

Themes such as these run deep in Hebrew memory. They bring strength in times of weakness and hope in times of trial. The Bible is the Jewish community's inspiration. The memory of the Exodus is imbedded in the liturgy, or the rites of public worship, of the Jewish people. The third evening blessing in the weekday liturgy repeats this memory:

> *All this is true and trustworthy, and we firmly hold that He is the Lord our God, beside Whom no other god exists, and that we, Israel, are His people. He is the One Who delivered us from the hand of kings, our King, Who redeemed us from the power of all tyrants. He is the God Who . . . took vengeance on Pharaoh; Who in His anger smote all the firstborn of Egypt, and brought out His people Israel from among them to enjoy everlasting freedom; Who led His children through the divided Red Sea, but drowned their pursuers and enemies in its depths. Then His children saw His power; they praised and thanked His name, and willingly accepted His rule over them. Moses and the children of Israel sang to the Lord with great joy, and they all said, "Who is like You, O Lord, among the mighty ones? Who is like You, majestic in holiness, revered in praises, working wonders?"* (Exodus 15:11) *Your children saw Your royal power when You split open the Red Sea before Moses. They exclaimed, "He is my God."* (Exodus 15:2) *They said, "The Lord shall reign for ever and ever."* (Exodus 15:18)

The story of the Exodus carries within it the memory of the plagues sent by God to convince Pharaoh to free the Jews. The

above benediction recalls the sending of the Angel of Death by God to slay all the firstborn in the land of Egypt. The Angel of Death passed over the houses of the children of Israel and did not bring death to them. Each year this event and its importance is commemorated by the festival of Passover, which celebrates the escape of the Jews from Egypt and stirs Jewish hearts to thank the God who saved them. The *Haggadah shel Pesah* (the Narration of the Passover), read solemnly in Jewish homes each year at Passover, declares

> *This is the bread of affliction which our fathers ate in the land of Egypt. Let all who are hungry come eat; let all who are in need come to our Passover feast. Now we are here; next year may we be in the land of Israel! Now we are slaves; next year may we be free! We were Pharaoh's slaves in Egypt, but the Lord our God brought us out from there with a strong hand and an outstretched arm. If the Holy One, blessed be He, had not brought our fathers out from Egypt, then we, our children, and our children's children would still be Pharaoh's slaves in Egypt. So even though all of us were wise, all of us clever, all of us elders, all of us knowledgeable in the Torah, yet we would be duty-bound to tell the story of the coming out of Egypt. The more a man tells the story of the coming out from Egypt, the more he is to be praised.*

The theme of deliverance from slavery indicated by such benedictions and prayers runs deep in the Jewish tradition and in Hebrew awareness. The prophet Hosea, speaking for God, reminds the Israelites that God, with the care of a father, delivered their ancestors from the slavery of Egypt: "When Israel was a child, I loved him, and out of Egypt I called my son." (Hosea 11:1) He reinforces the same memory when speaking for God again: "I am the Lord your God from the land of Egypt; you know no God but Me, and besides Me there is no savior." (Hosea 13:4) Again, deliverance is a theme during the time of the Exile. And it is a theme often sounded in prayers asking God to deliver the petitioner or the Jewish community from the moral enslavement that weakens it.

The theme of wandering in the wilderness likewise runs deep in Biblical literature and in the Jewish soul. In its most forceful sense, this theme is based on the forty years of wandering by Moses and the Hebrew people as they fled Egypt and marched toward the Promised Land. This story is one of the central events recounted in Exodus and Numbers. In fact, the title of the Book of Numbers in Hebrew is the opening word of the book, *Bemidbar*, which means "in the wilderness." The hardships and difficulties of those years of wandering in the desert, often without food or drink, have been a constant support to Jews who have faced similar difficulties through the ages.

But the theme of wandering long predates the wandering in the wilderness. The very word *Hebrew* probably comes from the word *Habiru*, or *Apiru*, which means "wanderer" or "outsider." Furthermore, the father of the Hebrews was Abraham, a wanderer who took his cattle from place to place for grazing, and whose first command from God was "Go from your country and your kindred and your father's house to the land that I will show you." He left his home in Chaldea and spent endless years searching for the promised land. Abraham's descendants have very often followed in his wandering footsteps. Moses escaped the slavery of Egypt, then wandered for forty years in the desert. Considering the history of the Jewish people (Chapters 2 and 3), it is not difficult to realize how often the wanderings of their fathers, Abraham and Moses, have been repeated in the lives of their children and their children's children, down through the ages.

These events recorded in the Torah live in the hearts and liturgies of the Jewish people, and the great figures of the Pentateuch stand out in their memory. Abraham is a powerful example of a person with deep trust in God. His trials were many, and one in particular stands out—God's command to him to sacrifice his son, Isaac. The story, recounted in Genesis, indicates that "Abraham rose early in the morning, saddled his beast, and took two of his young men with him, and his son Isaac . . ." (Genesis 22:3) This verse shows Abraham's readiness to follow God's command. When they arrived at the moment of sacrifice,

■ *The wandering Abraham had many trials throughout his life. The greatest was God's request that he sacrifice his son, Isaac. In this drawing we see him marching obediently with Isaac to the altar of sacrifice.*

Then Abraham put forth his hand, and took the knife to slay his son. But the angel of the Lord called to him from heaven, and said, "Abraham, Abraham!" And he said, "Here am I." He said, "Do not lay your hand on the lad or do anything to him; for now I know that you fear God, seeing you have not withheld your son, your only son, from me." (Genesis 22:10–12)

This story has had a powerful hold on both Jewish and Christian imaginations. In an early Jewish commentary from about the seventh century C.E., the author vividly interprets the scene:

> *Then Abraham stretched out his hand and took the knife to sacrifice his son. Isaac answered and said to his father: "Bind me well so that I may not struggle in the anguish of my soul, lest a blemish be found in your offering, and I be cast into the pit of destruction." The eyes of Abraham looked at the eyes of Isaac, but the eyes of Isaac looked at the angels on high; Isaac saw them, but Abraham did not see them. The angels on high answered: "Come and see these two unique men on the earth. One sacrifices and the other is victim; the one who sacrifices does not hesitate; the one to be sacrificed stretches out his neck."*
> (Targum Pseudo–Jonathan, 10)

Such imaginative meditations on each scene of this Torah story have been frequent in Jewish and Christian history and literature. Just this one aspect of Abraham's life has provided, over the centuries, spiritual reflection that has deeply influenced attitudes of many people during times of trial and suffering.

Exodus, Leviticus, Numbers, and Deuteronomy establish the laws for Israel. The Ten Commandments (Exodus 20) give the over-arching guidelines for Israelite behavior with respect to God and to fellow humans. These are universal principles of behavior that create the framework for a moral and ethical society dedicated to God. The last book of the Torah—the Book of Deuteronomy, or the second telling of the Law—captures the essence of the relationship between God and Israel. Moses instructs the Israelites to follow God's laws because God loves them. They, in turn, must love him. In the "Shema" (Deuteronomy 6:4–9) Moses declares:

> *Hear, O Israel, the Lord our God is one Lord. You shall love the Lord your God with all your heart, and with all your soul, and with all your might. And these words*

which I command you this day shall be upon your heart;
and you shall teach them diligently to your children,
and shall talk of them when you sit in your house, and
when you walk by the way, and when you lie down and
when you rise. And you shall bind them as a sign upon
your hand, and they shall be as frontlets between your
eyes. And you shall write them on the doorposts of your
house and on your gates. (Deuteronomy 6:4–9)

Elsewhere the Torah establishes rules for justice and love among the people of Israel:

You will not be unjust in administering justice. You
will neither be partial to the poor nor overawed by the
great, but will administer justice to your fellow citizen
justly. You will not go about slandering your own
family, nor will you put your neighbor's life in jeopardy.
I am Yahweh. You will not harbor hatred for your
brother. . . . You will not exact vengeance on, or bear any
sort of grudge against, the members of your race, but
you will love your neighbor as yourself. I am Yahweh.
     (Leviticus 19:15–18)

The Torah, with its events and characters, has provided the foundation of deep religious faith in the Jews for more than 2,500 years. The Law given to Moses, recorded in the books of Exodus, Leviticus, and Deuteronomy, has guided Jewish life since Mosaic times and is the ultimate authority on all matters of belief and practice for Judaism.

The Prophets (*Nebiyim*)

The Early Prophets trace the history begun in the Torah from the period of the Conquest through the Divided Monarchy (see Chapter 2). Traditionally attributed to the prophets Joshua, Samuel, and Jeremiah, these books describe the relationship between God and Israel while Israel was evolving as a nation. The primary themes are Israel's success when it is obedient to the Law of God given to Moses and its suffering when it is disobedient.

The Later Prophets include the preachings of a number of individuals in different times during the Monarchy, the Exile,

and the Restoration. The prophets are described as specially chosen by God to be his spokespersons to the king and the people. This was not always an easy task. It often entailed direct confrontation with powerful kings, political leaders, or even official prophets who worked as pawns of the powerful political leaders. The difficulties of the task can be seen in the first response of Jeremiah to his appointment as a prophet of God:

> *Now the word of the Lord came to me saying, "Before I formed you in the womb I knew you, and before you were born I consecrated you; I appointed you a prophet to the nations." Then I said, "Ah, Lord God! Behold, I do not know how to speak, for I am only a youth." But the Lord said to me, "Do not say, 'I am only a youth'; for to all to whom I send you you shall go, and whatever I command you you shall speak. Be not afraid of them, for I am with you to deliver you." (Jeremiah 1:5–8)*

While the prophets differed in the scope and detail of their visions, their works elaborated on the teachings of the Torah and reshaped the religious thought of ancient Israel. Three main themes run through the prophets' teachings: the monotheism of God, morality, and the coming of a glorious future (see Chapter 2). Yahweh was, for the prophets, not just the God of Israel, but the single, universal, holy God who controlled all nations, history, and nature. Even though he was a mystery and was removed from the world, he had a special bond with Israel.

The special relationship between Israel and God required Israel to be held to a higher moral standard than other nations. The prophets understood obedience to the law as the way to create a just and fair world. Their messages were strongly critical of the neglect of the Law or challenged the mechanical fulfillment of its demands through sacrifices and rituals. The words of the prophet Amos, who attacks the Israelites' behavior in the name of God, illustrate the moral teachings of the prophets:

> *They hate him who reproves in the gate, and they abhor him who speaks the truth. Therefore, because you trample upon the poor and take from him of wheat, you have*

built houses of hewn stone, but you shall not dwell in them; you have planted pleasant vineyards, but you shall not drink their wine. For I know how many are your transgressions, and how great are your sins— you who afflict the righteous, who take a bribe, and turn aside the needy at the gate. Therefore, he who is prudent will keep silent in such a time; for it is an evil time. Seek good, and not evil, that you may live. (Amos 5:10–14)

In their accent on the moral character of life, the prophets have become an influence today in both traditional and modern forms of Judaism. The prophets call the traditional Jews back to the Law and to the purer observance of it. They also stimulate the modern forms of Judaism to pursue justice, to help the needy overcome poverty, and to aim at establishing equality.

The Writings (*Ketubiyim*)

The Writings includes the "wisdom books"—Job, Proverbs, and Ecclesiastes—and other literature related to the Hebrew Bible as a whole. The wisdom books explore questions of human existence, such as how to lead a good and happy life (Ecclesiastes) and how to understand apparent contradictions in the order of God's world (Job). Other texts in the Writings give examples of proper conduct (Proverbs) or courageous behavior (Esther, Daniel, and Ezra-Nehemiah), or make human characteristics or institutions seem legitimate within the structure of the world as defined in the rest of the Hebrew Bible (Lamentations).

The Writings also includes the Book of Psalms, which bears the Hebrew name Tehillim, meaning "Praises." These Praises are songs of adoration, thanksgiving, confession, and petition, manifesting joy, sorrow, and confidence in life. The Praises always declare the glory of God, no matter what their mood. Their beauty is stunning and simple, as we can see in the Shepherd's Psalm:

The Lord is my shepherd, I shall not want. He makes me lie down in green pastures; He leads me beside still waters. He restores my soul; He leads me in paths of righteousness for His name's sake. Even though I walk through the valley of the shadow of death, I fear no

A rabbi deep in meditation on the text of the Talmud.

evil; for Thou art with me; Thy rod and Thy staff, they comfort me. Thou preparest a table before me in the presence of my enemies; Thou anointest my head with oil. My cup overflows. Surely goodness and mercy shall follow me all the days of my life; and I shall dwell in the house of the Lord for ever. (Psalm 23:1–6)

The Bible as Literature

Aside from its religious importance, the Hebrew Bible is one of the greatest and most influential literary works of the Western world. Its compilers, those who put it together bit by bit, attempted to be all-encompassing. It thus accounts for nearly every aspect of human existence. Moreover, much of its prose and poetry is masterful and elegant, and nearly every genre of literature is represented within the text. Over the centuries, the events, the figures, and the message of the Hebrew Bible have inspired other great works in the areas of art, music, literature, and philosophy.

CHAPTER **5**

Branches of Judaism and Their Basic Beliefs

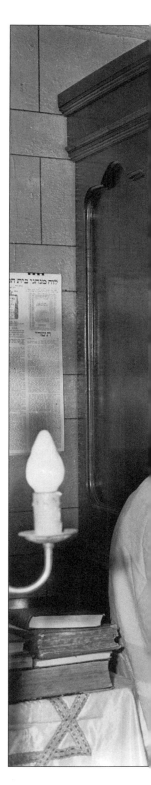

*T*he basic beliefs of Judaism are outlined in the first chapter of this book. They include the following principles:

1. There is only one God. He controls the events of nature and history according to his divine design, which is beyond our comprehension.

2. God chose Abraham and his descendants as his special people and promised that they would be a great nation dwelling in the Promised Land (Canaan).

3. God made a covenant with the Hebrews at Mount Sinai where he gave the Law to the people through Moses. The Law provides the rules by which the faithful are to live.

4. Abraham's people were chosen to be the model of behavior for all nations in the future age of the Messiah, who will rule the world in peace and justice.

During the history of the Jews, these principles have been interpreted in different ways, and a number of branches of Judaism have developed.

The Impact of Rabbinical Judaism

The work of the rabbis in the era 70–640 C.E., discussed in Chapter 3, adapted the Biblical faith that was centered on the Temple and on Jerusalem to the need of the Jews in a new situation outside of Jerusalem after the destruction of the Temple. The rabbis took on a way of life that showed faithfulness to God. They taught that this faithful way of life should be lived by all Jews. In this sense, every Jew possessed priestly qualities because the rituals that had previously been carried out in the Temple were now also carried out at home or in the workplace. At home, the table became an altar; anything that came to it had to be kosher, or ritually acceptable. When the men went to work, a special fringe on the corner of their clothing reminded them of their responsibilities to God. Daily study of the Torah, the Mishnah, the Talmud, and the Midrash was encouraged.

The Jewish family and its life became the central focus, although there was always a tendency to try to join with other families to form a broader community. The broader Jewish community centered around several unifying institutions: the synagogue as the place of prayer, the study house as a meeting place for students of the Torah, and the rabbinical court as a protector of the community's spiritual well-being. These institutions brought cohesion to the Jews of late antiquity.

Sefardic Judaism

When Judaism spread throughout the Near East, North Africa, and into Spain, Spain became the center of Jewish learning and culture during the Middle Ages. Spanish Jewish culture attained a very high level, especially in the eleventh and twelfth centuries. One of the greatest figures during this period was Moses Maimonides. He expressed the creed of the Sefardic Jews in thirteen basic beliefs:

1. Yahweh alone is the Creator.
2. Yahweh is absolutely One.
3. Yahweh has no body or bodily shape.
4. Yahweh is the first and the last.
5. Only to Yahweh may we pray and to no other.
6. The words of the prophets are true.

7. The prophecy of Moses is true, and he is the father of all prophets.
8. The Torah, now found in our hands, was given to Moses.
9. This Torah is not subject to change, and there will never be another Torah from the Creator.
10. The Creator knows all the thoughts and deeds of humans.
11. Yahweh rewards and punishes according to the deed.
12. The Messiah will come; though He tarry, I will expect Him daily.
13. The dead will be resurrected.

Some of his Jewish contemporaries attacked Maimonides' creed. They felt that his theoretical beliefs were foreign to the practical way of life underscored by rabbinic Judaism. They also saw his creed as an attempt to imitate the Christian creeds. Despite these objections to Maimonides' creed, it was passed on as a statement of traditional Jewish beliefs and has even been cast into a poetic hymn, the *Yigdal*, which is used in public worship.

The Sefardic Jews were expelled from Spain in 1492 and settled in North Africa, Egypt, Syria, Italy, and in the provinces of the Turkish Empire, especially Salonika and Istanbul. Later, they established communities in a number of European cities: London, Amsterdam, Hamburg, and Bordeaux. They spoke a Judeo-Spanish language called Ladino and developed a significant Ladino literature. In the modern division of Jewish groups, Sefardic Jews are usually contrasted with Ashkenazic Jews. The label "Sefardic," has come to describe all Jews who are non-Ashkenazic.

Ashkenazic Judaism

The Ashkenazic Jews followed the geographical path of the Roman legions, settling in Italy, France, Germany, Britain, and then moving into Poland and Russia. Frequently, the medieval Ashkenazic Jews lived in circumstances that kept their culture separated from the rest of the world. They became one community by their strengthening conviction that they were the chosen

people of Yahweh's covenant. Unlike the Sefardic Jews, Ashkenazic Jews did not participate strongly in the culture and sophisticated social life of well-educated, non-Jewish people.

The Ashkenazic Jews were people of traditional religious practices. They followed the demands of Torah (Law) and Mitzvot (Commandments). One of the Ashkenazic leaders, Joseph Karo (1488–1575), encouraged them to observe these rituals strictly in order to remain unified. He called this strict observance the *Shulhan Arukh* (the Well-Prepared Table). With additions and adjustments (called The Tablecloth) by his young follower, Moses Isserles (1530–1572), the *Shulhan Arukh* became and remains the code of traditional Ashkenazic Jews.

While the Sefardic Jews spoke Ladino, the Ashkenazic Jews spoke Yiddish. Ashkenazic rituals were closely linked to the ancient Palestinian tradition—those of the Jewish people in their homeland. In contrast, the Sefardic Jews reached back to the ancient Babylonian tradition that was developed by Jews in exile. Of the Jews exterminated during the Holocaust, the vast majority were Ashkenazic: their numbers fell from 15 million before World War II, to about 9.5 million after. Today, Ashkenazic Jews outnumber Sefardic Jews by a ratio of four to one.

Reform Judaism

Judaism entered a new world after the Enlightenment, which was to a great extent an effort to lessen the importance of religious differences. The Jews thus gained emancipation from religion-dominated states. They were called to an awareness of their humanity, not specifically to their Jewishness. The thinking during the Enlightenment also called for Jewish worship and practices to be brought in line with the human culture of its surroundings and the universal characteristics common to all religions. Could a religion that so strongly stressed the special character of the Jews as God's people—with a unique mission "to the nations"—continue to exist in Western European countries like France, Germany, and England? In these countries, Jews would now have equal citizenship with people who belonged to other religions, or to no religion at all. Could hopes for a Messiah, for the rebuilding of the Temple, or for a return to

a homeland with Jerusalem as its capital, live on in the Jewish person with citizenship in a modern Diaspora land? Abraham Geiger (1810–1874), the founder of Reform Judaism, offered a philosophical perspective to guide the modern Jews.

Geiger thought that traditional beliefs might be more readily accepted in modern Western society if the focus of Judaism was given a new meaning. He suggested that instead of a personal Messiah, Jews await the coming of the Messianic age characterized by equality, freedom, and human brotherhood. This interpretation of Judaism would not only give Jews a set of ideals to be proud of, but also would transform Judaism into a religion that non-Jews could surely admire. For Geiger, this was the genius of the Jews: they always practiced an ethical, or moral and just, religion; they had always carried their ethical values to the rest of humanity. According to Geiger, the temple that needed to be rebuilt was not an actual building in Jerusalem; it was an ideal spiritual structure of values, of justice, and of freedom. Furthermore, Jerusalem was not a physical place, but a place of ethical values rooted deeply and personally within Jewish hearts in all lands.

Early Reform Judaism was therefore opposed to Zionism, whose followers dreamed of a literal Jewish homeland—a return to the Promised Land. From the Reform viewpoint, the Zionist movement clung too strongly to an old-fashioned Messianism and a separatist viewpoint. Reform Judaism began to support Zionism only when the Zionist movement's hope for a return to their homeland became an effort to construct a modern state with modern attitudes, where the Jewish people could fulfill their mission of spiritualizing mankind by examples of openness and enlightenment.

In Europe, Reform Judaism paved the way for Jewish integration within society. The Reform Jews' respect for human dignity and their serious ethical concern for justice and equality made them good citizens as well as religious Jews. Through their beliefs, Reform Jews showed other citizens that they shared the common pursuit of moral values.

In America, the beliefs and structures of Reform Judaism arose from the experiences of early American Jews. These Jews

first integrated into mainstream American society, then searched for a theory within their religion to state what they had accomplished. Changes in their rituals of worship were modest, mainly requiring that English be used out of consideration for worshipers who no longer understood Hebrew or German. In 1855, David Einhorn arrived in Baltimore from Germany and attempted to direct American Judaism by establishing a German form of Reform Judaism. He tried to use the well-defined ideas of the German form of Enlightenment Jewry to get American Jews to follow the ethical goals of modern Enlightenment Judaism. However, Reform Judaism was happening in the United States more as a natural development of living in this country, not as a set of conclusions from theoretical premises.

In 1873, Isaac Wise organized a Union of American Hebrew Congregations in Cincinnati. Two years later, Hebrew Union College, a Union-sponsored Reform seminary for training rabbis, was established. Without official action, Reform Judaism had achieved its goal: the Jews in 1880 had become Americanized and, without great fanfare, they had modified their ritual practices to reflect the tastes of Jewish people who wanted respectability in a country where they felt at home.

A formal definition of Reform Judaism in America came only after the changes in Judaism had taken place within American society. In 1885, Kaufman Kohler, the son-in-law of David Einhorn, held a conference of rabbis in Pittsburgh. At the conference, he proposed a Jewish platform that would be broad, compassionate, enlightened, and liberal enough to impress and win the hearts of Americanized Jews:

> It will not do to offer our prayers in a tongue which only few scholars nowadays understand. We cannot afford any longer to pray for a return to Jerusalem. It is a blasphemy and lie upon the lips of every American Jew. We accept as binding only its [the Scriptures] moral laws, but reject all such as are not adapted to the views of modern civilization.

In 1881, vast numbers of Ashkenazic Jews began to arrive in America. The result was that the proportion of Reform Jews was

greatly reduced by around 1915. In an effort to keep Judaism in the United States from falling back into the more traditional and foreign elements of the Ashkenazic Jews, the Reform Judaism movement began to portray itself as dedicated to reform and change. Reform rabbis endorsed the Columbus Platform of 1937. This platform describes Reform Judaism's embrace of both traditional concepts and commitments to adapting timely change:

> *Judaism is the historical religious experience of the Jewish people. . . . the Torah, both written and oral, enshrines Israel's ever-growing consciousness of God and of the moral law. It preserves the historical precedents, sanctions and norms of Jewish life. . . . Being products of historical processes, certain of its laws have lost their binding force with the passing of conditions that called them forth. But, as a depository of Israel's spiritual ideals, the Torah remains the dynamic source of the life of Israel. Each age has the obligation to adapt the teachings of the Torah to its basic needs in accordance with the genius of Judaism.*

Reform Judaism Today

Reform Judaism stresses the reasonableness of Judaism. It represents Judaism as a progressive religion, striving for harmony with reason. Reform Jews reject what they consider to be the antiquarian ideas of Biblical language and thought. Their religious outlook also had rejected Zionism. They felt that Zionism's demand to establish a Jewish nation might split the loyalty of Jewish people in the countries in which they live. The main commitment of Reform Judaism is not so much to a collection of beliefs, but to the affirmation of the ethical character of Judaism: its dedication to justice and liberty, wherever Jews may live.

Today, Reform Judaism, especially in the United States and Israel, plays an important role within the Jewish community, as well as in the broader political world. In the United States, Reform Judaism counts more than 2 million members, or 42 percent of American Jews. Its influence flows into many areas of life, through its pursuit of ethical objectives and promotion of change.

Changes Introduced by Reform Judaism

In general, this modernizing form of Judaism has emphasized "decorum," or suitable behavior, in worship. Reform Jews rejected services conducted solely in Hebrew, which often caused uncomprehending congregations to mill around, talking in a manner that was embarrassingly inappropriate. Religious services of Reform Jews frequently followed the models of contemporary Christian Protestant congregations. Reform Jews adapted innovative changes to the old forms of worship, such as seating families together instead of segregating males and females. They also incorporated organs and choirs and discarded the traditional marks of male piety such as the *yarmulke* (skullcap) and the *tallit* (prayer shawl). The native tongue became the language of worship. Innovative sermons were preached in the vernacular, or common language, not in Hebrew. Even the role of the rabbi changed from scholar of the Torah and Talmud to that of preacher, adviser, and administrator. Contrary to Orthodox tradition, Reform Judaism decided in 1972 to allow the ordination of women rabbis. Sally Priesand was the first woman rabbi ordained by a Jewish theological seminary, the Hebrew Union College. Reform Jews also determined that the child of either a Jewish father or a Jewish mother should be considered a Jew. They also eased restrictions concerning conversion of non-Jews and rules governing the marriage between Jews and non-Jews.

Reform Judaism Facing Its Challenges

As mentioned above, Reform Judaism originally rejected Zionism's call for a Palestinian homeland. However, with growing anti-Semitism in Europe on the eve of World War II, Reform Jews adapted their position to the changing realities. The Columbus Platform of 1937 manifests this alteration:

> *Judaism is the soul of which Israel is the body. . . . In the*
> *rehabilitation of Palestine . . . we affirm the obligation of*
> *all Jewry to aid in its upbuilding as a Jewish homeland. . . .*

Frequently, other Jews have charged Reform Judaism with abandoning traditional religious principles, of betraying many

of the riches of the Jewish memory, of disrespecting the nonethical aspects of religion, and of flippantly rejecting all traditional religion. Just as Reform Jews adapted to the call for a Jewish homeland, today they are also beginning to see ways of giving new meanings to some of the traditions of the past. A recent survey by the Union of American Hebrew Congregations indicates that Reform Judaism has revived many earlier Judaic practices. These include providing men with yarmulkes, kindling the Sabbath candles before Friday evening services, reciting blessings before and after readings from the Torah at Sabbath morning services, and observing two days of the Rosh Hashanah holiday. The director of the survey commission was careful to point out that this is not a return to Orthodox Judaism, but the expression of a post-Holocaust generation of Reform Jews who are seeking new dimensions of Jewish spirituality.

Orthodox Judaism

As a response to the growth of Reform Judaism in Europe, Moses Sofer (1762–1839), a rabbi from Bratislava, in present-day Slovakia, called on all traditional Jews to make no compromise with modernity. He summoned them to keep themselves separate from reform-dominated communities if they did not want to lose their Jewish identity. His appeal was heard and promoted by many traditional rabbis, such as Samson Raphael Hirsch (1808–1888), of Oldenburg, Germany. Hirsch, though traditional in his beliefs, was a person who was not afraid to use modern methods for communicating the traditional message. He fostered Orthodox newspapers and political parties.

With the immigration into the United States of more than 1,750,000 Jews between 1881 and the beginning of World War I, the Reform movement of Judaism diminished because, for the most part, the immigrants were traditional Jews. They were poor and not highly educated. By establishing the Jewish Theological Seminary in New York City in 1885, traditional American Jews tried to help these immigrants adapt to American life and to preserve their religious traditions. But their efforts to raise the level of religious study, to maintain standards of observance, and to exercise authority met with little success. There was just too

■ *A student reflecting on a page of the Talmud, the written and oral law that guides Jewish life.*

much of a gap between the cultured, English-speaking American Orthodox Jews and the new immigrants.

Other Orthodox efforts were made toward the turn of the century, such as the establishment of the first *yeshiva* (academy), called the Rabbi Isaac Elchanan Theological Seminary. Even though the seminary was successful later and became the basis of Yeshiva University, it was not very effective in the opening decades of the twentieth century. Efforts to organize a Union of Orthodox Jewish Congregations were made in 1898, and a Union of Orthodox Rabbis was formed in 1902. However, none of these institutions was able to become the center for the religious life of the Eastern European Jews who immigrated here.

The vacuum that remained after these unsuccessful efforts was occupied by a number of substitute organizations—Jewish trade unions, fraternal organizations that gathered people from the same European locale, the Jewish press, and the Yiddish theater. But traditional Jews were looking for something more than a social approach to Jewish unity; they were looking for a religious basis. They therefore gravitated toward Orthodox

Judaism, which maintained that traditional Jewish laws should continue to be followed, even by modern-day Jews.

In recent years, some Orthodox Jews have promoted a new form of Orthodoxy in America. This seems to be part of a more modern conservative, or traditional, thrust in Jewish culture. In an effort to forge a deeper religious unity, Orthodox Judaism has formed a progressive movement that has been described as Neo-Orthodoxy. The works of Samson Raphael Hirsch are its religious foundation. As more women and men of business and intellectual achievement gave their support to this modern form of traditional Judaism, it expanded its school system, established a network of congregations, and produced a literature that strengthens and deepens traditional religious unity within a modern American context.

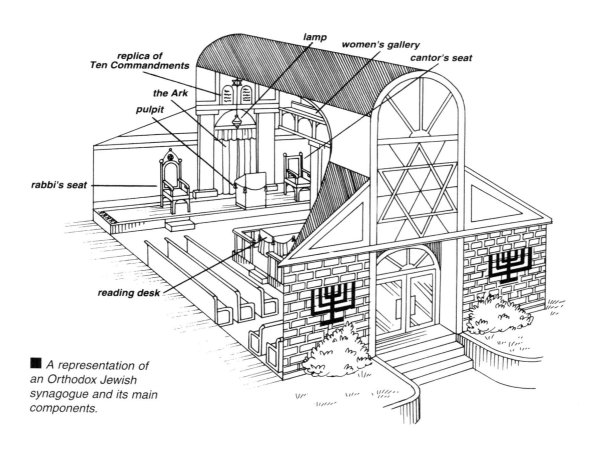

A representation of an Orthodox Jewish synagogue and its main components.

Of the 13 million Jews in the world today, about 2 million belong to the various forms of Orthodoxy. Of these, about 350,000 live in the United States. In Israel, Orthodox Jews are divided mainly between the Ashkenazic and the Sefardic Orthodox Jews. Each of these two forms of Orthodox Judaism has its own chief rabbi. Although, in both the United States and Israel, Orthodox Jews play an influential religious role within the Jewish community, they are in the minority with respect to Reform and Conservative Jews and have less influence on non-Jewish society.

Orthodox Judaism and Its Practices Today

Orthodox Judaism teaches that traditional Jewish law, as given to Moses by Yahweh in the form of the Torah, is the ultimate religious authority that binds all Jews. Modern interpretations of the Bible that treat sacred Jewish works as mythical or fictional history are rejected as irreverent. Yet, even among Orthodox Jews, there are significant differences. Those from Eastern Europe generally oppose all innovation in language, dress, and education, while those from Western Europe favor, or at least accept, modern dress, and use of the vernacular, and permit the pursuit of secular education.

■ **Kosher ("clean") foods, which can be eaten:**

Cow (cattle)	Turkey
Lamb	Chicken
Duck	Bass
Goose	Cod
Pheasant	Tuna

Treyf ("unclean") foods, which cannot be eaten:

Pig	Lobster
Eel	Oyster
Catfish	Scallops
Shark	Shrimp
Clams	Squid

■ *A customer, mindful of the strict dietary and religious rules to be observed during Passover, examines the meat cases at Ventura Kosher Meats in Tarzana, California.*

In addition to reverence for the Torah and Talmud, Orthodox Jews follow *Kashrut* (a dietary code) with great seriousness. They eat only *kosher* (ritually clean) foods listed in the book of Leviticus. Some important features of this dietary code are that pork and shellfish are *treyf* (not fit to eat); fish must have both scales and fins; meat and dairy products are not to be mixed; and a kosher kitchen should have two sets of dishes—one for dairy and one for meat. Even animals that are fit to eat must be slaughtered in a special manner.

Orthodox Jews pray daily, but the core of Jewish worship is weekly observance of the Sabbath. On the Sabbath all work stops. Meals and other necessities are prepared beforehand so that the entire day, from Friday at sunset to Saturday at sunset, can be dedicated to rest and worship.

Hasidism

As described in Chapter 3, in the twelfth century C.E., a group of *Hasidim,* very pious ascetics, arose in Ashkenazic communities. A similar revivalist movement was formed in Eastern Europe around a charismatic teacher, Israel Ba'al Shem Tov (1699–1761), in the 1700s. Ba'al Shem Tov, or Besht as he was called, preached that God was present everywhere, and that it was the task of religious Jews to achieve *devekut*—continual communion with God—in all that they did. The spiritual teacher, or *tzaddik*, was a rabbi who should lead his followers, usually simple and common people, to experience God in all things. Hasidim differed from other Orthodox Jews by their firm loyalty to their rabbis, who served as links between the divine and created world and brought God's blessings into the lives of the faithful followers.

Spiritual leadership was and continues to be crucial to Hasidic communities. These communities are collectives that center around their charismatic leaders. Two of the most famous followers of Rabbi Ba'al Shem Tov were Rabbi Dov Ber (1740–1773), who succeeded Besht and systematized his preaching and doctrine, and Rabbi Jacob Joseph (1848–1902). Rabbi Joseph presents a vivid example of the nature and role of a *tzaddik*—a rabbi who gained his authority through his contemplative life and his spiritual

■ *Touro Synagogue,
built between 1759–1763,
is the oldest synagogue
in the United States and
the only one remaining
from the colonial era.*

charisma rather than through the Talmudic learning that characterized the traditional rabbis. The spiritual leadership of the *tzaddik* was passed on in each Hasidic community as an inheritance that often followed the model of a spiritual dynasty.

Although vast numbers of Hasidic Jews were exterminated by the Nazis during World War II, there are an estimated 250,000 Hasidim in the world today. They can be found in England, France, Belgium, Switzerland, Austria, and Israel, and almost 200,000 live in the United States. The largest Hasidic group (numbering about 100,000) is the Lubavitch community that resides in Brooklyn, New York. The Hasidic movement continues to grow steadily, especially in the United States.

Conservative Judaism

Zacharias Frankel (1801–1875) inspired Conservative Judaism. Frankel knew Jewish history well, and considered Reform Judaism to be an alternative form of Judaism. His ideas influenced the direction that Solomon Schechter (1850–1915) gave to Conservative Judaism. According to Frankel and Schechter, the mandates established in the Torah and the Talmud must be followed, but followed within the context of a living tradition. In other words, the current generation of Jews ought to shape the character of Jewish life in harmony with, but not rigidly bound by, the Torah and Talmud.

Formally, Conservative Judaism began with the founding of the United Synagogue of America in 1913. It was meant to be a bridge between Orthodox Judaism and Reform Judaism. According to the Conservative Jews, Orthodox Judaism was too rigid and Reform Judaism too innovative, with little connection to the living history of the Jewish people. Conservative Jews sought a middle ground between extreme traditionalism and extreme liberalism. American Conservative Jews attempted to blend the richly historical Jewish tradition with the demands of the modern world in which the Jewish community lives.

The Guiding Philosophy of Conservative Judaism

Conservative beliefs respect and follow the Torah and the Talmud. As described in Chapter 3, the Talmud developed under

the changing circumstances of the rabbinic era as the Jewish community tried to adapt the Torah to different times and circumstances. This is what is required of Jews in each era and in different worlds: they must, within the framework of the Law, interpret what the Law demands of them in their present circumstances. Thus, Conservative Judaism reread the ancient works in terms of new conditions.

The Practices of Conservative Judaism

Many of the practices of Conservative Judaism are common to those of Orthodox Jews. Conservative Jews would claim, however, that their practices are less mechanical, or routine. Conservative Judaism also places a strong emphasis on Jewish community-building in the form of religious education for children, youth programs, women's groups, and adult education.

Conservative Judaism Facing Its Challenges

As they attempt to update the Law in terms of the demands of modern life, Conservative communities face tensions among themselves over what adaptations are proper. An example of such a conflict is found in the question of whether to ordain women as rabbis. Some congregations favored the ordination of women rabbis on the basis of equality of the sexes. Other congregations argued that this move is such a basic departure from tradition that it will create an even deeper split between Conservative Judaism and Orthodox Judaism. A Conservative convention finally approved the ordination of women rabbis in 1983, and in 1984 eighteen women were admitted to the Jewish Theological Seminary. In 1985, Amy Eilberg was ordained as the first Conservative woman rabbi. This debate over women's ordination and similar problems illustrates the type of challenges faced by a movement that tries to be both traditional and modern.

Other Forms of American Judaism

Though Reform, Orthodox, and Conservative Judaism remain the three main branches, other types of Judaism have also formed within America. Reconstructionism is a movement that sees Judaism as an ever-evolving special community of

people rather than a religion whose followers conform to the teaching and law judged to be revealed by God. Of all the branches of American Judaism, Reconstructionism, whose followers number about 50,000, is the only indigenous one.

Originally led by Mordecai M. Kaplan (1881–1983), it is a very modern and American form of Judaism. Kaplan, in *Judaism as a Civilization* (1934), stressed that modern Jews must realize that they are heirs to a great civilization that, throughout its history, pursued holiness and social justice. He pleaded for Jews to demonstrate their loyalty to their Jewish inheritance by developing their moral dimensions and creative abilities. This, he argued, is the lesson of the Bible. The Bible teaches that rituals originally followed as divinely ordered acts of obedience, later became expressions of commitment to spiritual values, especially those of pursuing social justice. Kaplan contended that all Jews are the heirs of this great spiritual culture. The study of Jewish history, he claimed, would lead Jews to realize that traditional views of the Torah needed to be expanded to include commitments to social justice, to enriched, meaningful forms of ritual, and to artistic creativity. Reconstructionist synagogues, he believed, should be flourishing centers of every facet of a renewed Jewish life. They should be houses of prayer and study, but also home to the arts and music, and even health-promoting hubs of physical activity.

The Reconstructionist philosophy has championed women's rights and also created the *bat mitzvah* ceremony for young women corresponding to the parallel ceremony for young men. The movement has offered a number of other innovations within the Jewish world. One new declaration is that the child of a Jewish father and a non-Jewish mother is considered to be Jewish. The Reconstructionist Rabbinical College, which opened in Philadelphia in 1968, also ordained Sandy Eisenberg Sasso a rabbi in 1974. Reconstructionism is a modern, purely American movement that has had a strong influence on Reform and Conservative Jews, and has drawn into its fold Jews who tend to be secular.

CHAPTER 6

Rites of Passage

*T*he Jewish people celebrate four *mitzvot* (commandments) of their religion: circumcision, *bar* or *bat mitzvah* (meaning son or daughter of commandment), marriage, and death. Each mitzvah is a religious ritual for an essential event of human life: introduction into the community, two milestones of growth, and death or departure from the community.

Circumcision

In many hospitals today, male babies from differing religious backgrounds are routinely circumcised for medical reasons. For the Jews, circumcision of male offspring is not a medical exercise; it is a religious covenant called *berit milah* (covenant of circumcision). It welcomes the infant into the Jewish religious community, renewing the covenant made by Abraham and making the child part of God's covenant people. The act of circumcision fulfills the command given by Yahweh to Abraham as recorded in Genesis 17:9–13:

> *God said to Abraham, "As for you, you shall keep*
> *My covenant, you and your descendants after you*

■ *Preceding page-
An informal moment
of joyous celebration
at the **bar mitzvah** of
a young man in a
Reform synagogue.*

*throughout their generations. . . . Every male among
you shall be circumcised . . . He that is eight days old
among you shall be circumcised; every male throughout
your generations . . . shall be circumcised. So shall My
covenant be in your flesh an everlasting covenant."*

Circumcision is traditionally performed in the synagogue before at least ten men (the minimum number required by Jewish law to form a community) on the eighth day after birth, even if that day is the Sabbath, a feast day, or a fast day such as Yom Kippur. It is such an important event that it may be postponed only if circumcision is a threat to the child's health. The preferred time for the ceremony is in the morning, to imitate Abraham's eagerness to fulfill the commandment.

The ceremony of circumcision begins as the godmother carries the baby boy into the synagogue. This signifies the child's initiation into the Jewish community. The people gathered in the synagogue welcome the infant, saying:

"Blessed be he that comes."

The godmother then passes the child to the godfather, who passes the infant to the *mohel* (ritual circumciser). When the actual circumcision has taken place, the father speaks the blessing:

*"Blessed are You, O Lord Our God, Ruler of
the Universe, Who has sanctified us with Your
commandments and commanded us to bring our
sons into the covenant of Abraham our Father."*

The community responds:

*"Just as he entered the covenant, so may he enter into
the study of Torah, into marriage, and into good deeds."*

Customarily, the infant is named at this point in the ceremony. Then, a cup of wine is blessed by the *mohel*. With a prayer for happiness, a little wine is given to the infant; then the rest of the wine is finished by the father. A festive meal follows the ceremony.

In the different Jewish communities of today, many additions and adaptations have been made to this basic ceremony.

Reform Jews, for example, have introduced the ceremony *berit ha-hayyim* (covenant of life) to welcome female children into the community of covenant people. This ceremony does not include a surgical procedure, but it does use the basic language of the circumcision ceremony. The community welcomes the child, saying,

"Blessed is she who comes."

The mother speaks the blessing:

"Blessed is the Lord our God, Ruler of the Universe, by Whose mitzvot we are hallowed, Who commands us to sanctify life."

The father lights a candle and speaks the blessing:

"Blessed is the Lord, Whose Presence gives light to all the world."

Then the parents recite these words together:

"Blessed is the Lord our God, Ruler of the Universe, for giving us life, for sustaining us and enabling us to reach this day of joy."

Such adaptations show not only Reform Judaism's efforts to bring new values and dimensions to traditional ceremonies, but also show how deeply rooted this rite of initiation is in Jewish life. Circumcision is practiced, without such formal ritual, even by Jews who have been highly assimilated into modern culture. Some secular or nonreligious Jews also perform the rite. To more traditional religious Jews, the synagogue is the preferred setting for its performance. However, in many communities, the *berit milah* or *berit ha-hayyim* is held at the home of the new parents.

Different customs reign with regard to naming children. Ashkenazic Jews usually name their children after deceased relatives. Sefardic Jews tend to name their children after living relatives or other persons. Customarily, outside the state of Israel, Jewish children are given two names—a Hebrew name, used for religious occasions, and a secular name, used in nonreligious contexts.

Bar Mitzvah and Bat Mitzvah

Jews value education highly. At age five, children begin to learn religious traditions, either at home or in the synagogue. Jewish education includes lessons in the Torah, the Talmud, and in Midrash. Jews believe that this learning is based on divine teachings and best prepares them for life. This view is expressed in Isaiah 54:13–15:

> *All your sons shall be taught by the Lord, and great shall be the prosperity of your sons. In righteousness you shall be established; you shall be far from oppression, for you shall not fear; and from terror, for it shall not come near you. If any one stirs up strife, it is not from Me; whoever stirs up strife with you shall fall because of you.*

To the Jews, religious education leads to religious maturity. With the passage to maturity a young man becomes *bar mitzvah* (a son of commandment). This celebration takes place on his thirteenth birthday. In other non-Jewish cultures, the age of thirteen is symbolic of physical maturity, or puberty. Jews believe that through proper education, this is also the time of spiritual maturity or responsibility. It is the time of a young man's coming-of-age.

Usually, the religious coming-of-age is celebrated in the synagogue, and the young man plays a large role in the worship service. He is invited to read from the Torah, speak the blessings, and recite portions from the Prophets. If he is well trained, he might also be invited to recite an original prayer or to give an explanation of some Biblical or Talmudic subject. The event is usually followed by a festive meal or party.

Since the 1940s, this ritual has been introduced for young women of the Reform Jewish community. *Bat mitzvah* (daughter of commandment) is celebrated on the young woman's twelfth or thirteenth birthday.

In the nineteenth century, Reform Judaism formed a ceremony of confirmation as a substitute for *bar mitzvah*. The age of responsibility is celebrated for both young Jewish women and men in a group setting. Usually the ritual takes place near the

■ *A young girl learning the ABCs (or aleph, beth, etc.) of the Hebrew alphabet.*

feast of Shavuot, commemorating the reception of and commitment to the Ten Commandments. More recently, Reform Jews who practice the traditional *bar mitzvah* ceremony and the *bat mitzvah* ceremony continue to celebrate confirmation around the age of sixteen. The age for celebrating this ceremony was set at sixteen because, at that age, young people can better understand the commitments to responsible living. In the last three decades, many Conservative Jews have added confirmation to their Jewish practices as a rite of passage.

Marriage

In the Jewish tradition, marriage is a sacred relationship ordained by God:

So God created man in His own image, in the image of God He created him; male and female He created them. And God blessed them, and God said to them, "Be fruitful and multiply, and fill the earth and subdue it; and have dominion over the fish of the sea and over the birds of the air and over every living thing that moves upon the earth." (Genesis 1:27–28)

Jews believe that this divine command, "Be fruitful and multiply," is a religious demand to bear children to increase the number of people dedicated to the worship of Yahweh. In return, Yahweh fulfills the promise that he made to Abraham—that he will be the father of a great nation. The prophet Hosea even saw his own marriage with Gomer as a parallel to the covenant of God with Israel:

And I will betroth you to me forever; I will betroth you to me in righteousness and in justice, in steadfast love, and in mercy. I will betroth you to me in faithfulness; and you shall know the Lord. (Hosea 2:19–20)

There are many religious and symbolic sides to traditional Judaism, and the significance of marriage is shown by the solemn character of its ritual. In the rabbinical tradition, marriage took place in three formal states: *shiddukhin* (engagement), *quiddushim* (betrothal), and *nissu'in* (marriage). Although today engagement has become a simple statement of the intent to marry, it had previously been a formally written and legally binding contract including time, place, dowry, and guarantee of financial support.

Betrothal was in earlier ages separated from the marriage ceremony by an entire year. There was a seriousness about the betrothal that made it equivalent to the marriage itself. The young woman was made sacred, meaning she was set apart and dedicated to her future husband. To symbolize this, she wore a veil that covered her face during this period. Today, one aspect

of the betrothal ceremony still survives in the Orthodox marriage rite of Ashkenazic Jews: the groom covers the bride's face with a veil. This formal ceremony has the Yiddish title of *bedeken* (veiling).

Today, Jewish marriage ceremonies incorporate elements of the traditional engagement and betrothal ceremonies. After the *bedeken*, the couple is led by their parents to the traditional *huppah* (canopy) where they are greeted by the rabbi, who recites betrothal blessings over the first cup of wine:

> *Blessed are You, O Lord our God, Ruler of the Universe, creator of the fruit of the vine. Blessed are You, O Lord our God, Ruler of the Universe, Who has sanctified us by Your commandments and commanded us concerning forbidden relationships, Who has forbidden unto us those to whom we are merely betrothed, but has permitted unto us those who are married to us by means of the wedding canopy and the sacred rites of marriage. Blessed are You, O Lord our God, Who sanctifies His people Israel by means of the wedding canopy and the sacred rites of marriage.*

The bride and groom share the cup of wine. Then the groom places a plain ring on the index finger of the bride's left hand while saying the words, "Behold, you are consecrated to me by this ring as my wife according to the law of Moses and Israel." By willingly accepting the ring, the bride gives her consent. The rabbi then reads the marriage contract, a remnant of the traditional engagement, that has been signed previously by both parties. Next, the rabbi recites the *sheva' berakhot* (wedding blessings) over a second cup of wine:

> *Blessed are You, O Lord our God, Ruler of the Universe, creator of the fruit of the vine.*

> *Blessed are You, O Lord our God, Ruler of the Universe, Who has created all things for His glory.*

> *Blessed are You, O Lord our God, Ruler of the Universe, creator of man.*

■ The groom drinks from the cup of wine he shares with his wife during the wedding ceremony under the traditional **huppah** (canopy).

Blessed are You, O Lord our God, Ruler of the Universe, Who has made man in Your image, after Your likeness, and has prepared for him, out of his own being a help-mate forever. Blessed are You, O Lord, Creator of man.

May she who was barren rejoice and exult when her children will be gathered in her midst in joy. Blessed are You, O Lord, who makes Zion rejoice through her children.

Grant perfect joy to these loving companions, even as of old You gladdened Your creation in the garden of Eden. Blessed are You, O Lord, Who makes bridegroom and bride rejoice.

Blessed are You, O Lord our God, ruler of the Universe, Who created joy and gladness, bridegroom and bride, mirth and exultation, pleasure and delight, love, harmony, peace and companionship. Soon, O Lord our God, may there be heard in the cities of Judah and in the streets of Jerusalem the voice of joy and gladness, the voice of the bridegroom and the voice of the bride, the jubilant voice of bridegrooms from their wedding canopies and of youths from their feasts of song. Blessed are You, O Lord, Who makes the bridegroom rejoice with the bride.

The bride and groom share this second cup as a symbol of the life they will share together. The marriage ceremony customarily ends with the breaking of a glass, which is a call to return to more reasonable behavior after the excessive joy of the celebration. It also is a reminder of the destruction of the First and Second Temples (586 B.C.E. and 70 C.E.) and the suffering that Jews bear in a life that is still not perfect.

The marriage ceremony has been modified by Reform and Conservative Judaism. For example, many Reform and Conservative communities have introduced a two-ring ceremony in which the bride also presents the groom with a ring while reciting the words, "Behold, you are consecrated to me by this ring as my husband according to the law of Moses and Israel." Reform Judaism also has omitted the formal reading of the traditional marriage contract. Reform Jews have even introduced a new, egalitarian contract into the ceremony.

Death and Mourning

In death, according to traditional Judaism, the body returns to the dust of the earth from which it came, and the spirit returns to God who gave it. The funeral rite has simple traditions: the burial takes place as quickly after death as possible, and the

deceased is clothed in a plain white garment and placed in a simple coffin. The ceremony itself consists of recited Psalms from the Hebrew Bible, a eulogy, and a memorial prayer.

Traditionally, the coffin is carried to the grave in a procession that stops seven times, while Psalm 91 is recited. The casket is then placed in the grave and covered with earth. The burial service includes the recitation of *Tsidduq ha-Din* (acclamation of God's justice), a memorial prayer, and the recitation of the *Kaddish*, a prayer that acknowledges God's rule and leaves the ultimate destiny of people in his hands:

> *Magnified and sanctified be His Great Name in the world which He has created according to His will. May He establish His kingdom during your life and during your days, and during the life of all the house of Israel, speedily and in the near future; and say 'Amen.' May His great name be blessed forever and ever. Blessed, praised, and glorified, exalted, extolled and honored, adored and lauded be the Name of the Holy One. Blessed be He Who is beyond all blessings and hymns, praises and songs that are uttered in the world; and say 'Amen.' May there be abundant peace from heaven, and life for us and for all Israel; and say 'Amen.' May He Who maketh peace in the heavens, make peace for us and for all Israel; and say 'Amen' . . .*

When the burial service concludes, the people form two lines through which the mourners pass. Those who are present comfort the mourners with the words, "May God comfort you." The official mourners consist of the father, mother, brother, sister, daughter, son, and spouse of the deceased. Mourning itself falls into three periods: *aninut*, *shiv'ah*, and *sheloshim*.

Aninut lasts from death to the time of the burial. At this time, mourners display their deep sorrow by tearing either their garments or a symbolic black cloth attached to their garments. They are excused from other religious obligations so that they may prepare for the funeral and the burial. During *aninut*, mourners refrain from eating meat, drinking wine, or performing other activities that might distract them from their respectful

task. When the mourners return home from the burial, they enter the period of *shiv'ah*. They light a candle that symbolizes the human soul and burns for the seven days of *shiv'ah*. After returning from the funeral, the mourners are served a meal of consolation that has been prepared by friends and relatives.

During the seven days of *shiv'ah*, mourners customarily stay at home and avoid work and social gatherings. Orthodox Jews sit on special low benches and refrain from shaving, cutting their hair, taking pleasurable baths, and pursuing other sensual pleasures. A select group of at least ten men gathers each morning and evening for mourning services, comforting the mourners.

The period of *sheloshim* continues from the end of the seventh day until the thirtieth day. Mourners may return to work, but they continue to avoid social gatherings. In the case of a daughter or son mourning the death of a parent, this period of mourning lasts for a full year.

On the anniversary of a person's death, mourners light a candle that is kept lit for twenty-four hours, give charity in memory of the deceased, and attend services at which they recite the *Kaddish*. Also, a memorial service is held as part of the holy-day observances on *Yom Kippur*, on the last day of Passover, on the feast of *Shavuot* (Feast of Weeks) and on the last day of *Sukkot* (Feast of Tabernacles).

As with the other important ceremonies, the rituals of death and mourning have been adapted to modern situations. Since families do not always live close to one another, for example, burial often has to be delayed so that all mourners can attend. Many funerals today take place in funeral chapels or at the graveside. Especially in Reform and Conservative Jewish communities, these rituals now fit the needs of the times.

These central human rites of passage—acceptance into a community, attaining responsibility, marrying, and dying—take on a sacred and symbolic character for Jews. Within their individual communities, Jews share the *mitzvot* (commandments) and commemorate the religious part of these significant life passages.

■ *Two vessels are sailing the seas; one setting out from sheltered harbor to unknown destination; the other returning from strenuous voyage. As the ship comes home the people rejoice. Even so is life. Yet we rejoice when birth sends out the child on the uncertain voyage of life, should we not find comfort when the ship finally reaches the sheltered harbor of God's peace?*

Shemot Rabba
(Midrash on **Exodus***)*
48:1

CHAPTER 7

The Impact of Judaism

*T*he living traditions of Jewish culture and religious observance have had a strong impact on the world in which we live. Judaism has influenced Western civilization in a multitude of ways. In particular, Judaism has had a profound impact upon two other major world religions—Christianity and Islam. These religions adopted and spread a number of Judaism's fundamental principles. Furthermore, Jews throughout the world have helped to advance the cultural, political, and economic development of their nations.

The Religious Impact

The first major contribution of Judaism to world religions is monotheism, the belief in one God. Some ancient religions had moved toward the idea of monotheism by the second millennium B.C.E., but the single god imagined in these ancient cultures lacked certain characteristics of the God of Israel. A number of factors make the God of Israel unique:

1. He transcends—that is, he is separate from—the natural and human worlds. Indeed, he is the creator of the universe and everything in it.

2. God is universal. Not limited by time, geography, or human circumstances, he is present everywhere.

3. He is all-knowing and all-powerful.

4. Although he is separate from his creation, he is involved with it as the designer of the history of both natural and human events. His will can be read in natural phenomena, such as the fertility of the land or natural disasters, and in the social, political, and military histories of the nations. Further, as the judge of human behavior, he rewards the good and punishes the evil.

Judaism's second important contribution to religion is in the area of morality and ethics. Most of our commonly accepted norms for basic human rights and duties, ethical behavior, and justice come from the Law of Moses. For example, according to Jewish tradition, people have the intellectual ability and freedom of will to make choices about their conduct. Moreover, people have the responsibility to live a moral life because that is the purpose of human existence. To make the wrong choice or to avoid the moral challenge of life are immoral acts. These ideas are held to be true by many people in the world. One reason these ideas have been accepted and applied by many people is that they were originally proclaimed by Jewish belief to express God's will for a proper and correct human society.

The third important contribution to religion is in the area of ideas about serving one's community. Judaism teaches that people must account for the life that has been given to them—that is, God expects something in return for the creation of humanity. The tradition of charity and "good works" in the areas of education, health, and government, or any sort of community service, is fundamental to Judaism. This tradition became an integral part of Christianity and Islam.

Judaism also contributed a number of other basic features to later religions. A great many basic Christian ideas, such as the Messiah, the Day of Judgment, the Apocalypse, personal prayer, prayer services, spiritual purity, and the like, developed directly from Judaism. The idea of Scripture, or holy text, also originated

---

■ **The Meaning
of YHWH**

*The Jews had such
respect for God that
they did not pronounce
his name. The special
name that God gave
himself in Exodus 3:14
is **Ehyeh asher ehyeh:**
"I am who I am" or "I will
be who I will be." **Ehyeh**
is the first person
singular of the verb "to
be." YHWH is the third
person singular of the
same verb. YHWH thus
means "He is" or "He
will be," and is the first
word of the phrase "He
is who he is" or "He
will be who he will be."
Some English Bibles
out of respect for Jewish
religious tradition
translate it as "Lord"
or as "Jehovah."*

---

with Judaism. As the Scripture of the Jews, the Hebrew Bible became a source of the New Testament of the Christians. The Gospels of the New Testament, especially, have specific references to the prophecies of the Hebrew Bible. Christians also accept the Hebrew Bible as holy, and believe that it foreshadows many of the events in Jesus' life that are recorded in the New Testament.

To what extent Judaism directly influenced the formation of Islam and to what extent Christianity mediated it is not entirely clear. However, Judaism definitely contributed to the Islamic religion. Islam, too, derives its idea of holy text, the Koran, ultimately from Judaism. In addition, both the dietary and legal codes of Islam are based on those of Judaism. There is also evidence that the basic design of the Islamic house of worship, the mosque, comes from that of the early synagogues. Moreover, the communal prayer services of Islam and their devotional routines resemble those of Judaism.

Cultural Impact

As discussed in Chapter 1, the term *Jews* refers to both a religious and a cultural group living in many nations throughout the world. The Jews of the Diaspora have always participated in the wider cultural and political lives of the countries they inhabited. Jews, both practicing and non-practicing, have given exceptional contributions to the cultures of the nations in which they live. They have also contributed to western thought in nearly every area of human endeavor, including religion. It is testimony to the Jews' extraordinary contribution to intellectual endeavors that nearly one hundred people of Jewish descent have received the Nobel Prize for peace, literature, economics, physics, chemistry, and physiology or medicine since 1901.

The Arts

The Hebrew Bible contains many descriptions of works of art and architecture, especially the Temple of Solomon. These all suggest that ancient Israel had a rich artistic tradition, influenced, as all such traditions are, by the styles of neighboring nations. Down through the centuries, synagogues in Iraq,

■ *Moshe Safdie, a member of a leading architectural family in Israel, sits on the railing in front of Habitat, an apartment complex he exhibited at the 1967 Montreal World Exposition.*

Morocco, Spain, Italy, Germany, and the United States have had outstanding architectural designs. However, most of these buildings reflect the styles of the Christian or Muslim countries in which they were built. Most nineteenth-century American synagogues, for example, follow Greek Revival, Romanesque, and Gothic styles. Over the years, there have been efforts to interpret ancient Jewish forms and styles. Among the more recent are Norman Brunelli's stunning tentlike synagogue experiment, B'na i Jehudah, in Kansas City and Sidney Eisenshtat's Temple Mount Sinai in the desert setting of El Paso, Texas.

In the visual and graphic arts, themes from the Hebrew Bible and the life of the Diaspora have inspired both Jewish and non-Jewish artists in the West. This has been true since the

Middle Ages. Medieval cathedrals were richly decorated with sculptures of scenes from the Hebrew Bible. Michelangelo sculpted Moses and David and depicted Biblical scenes in his Sistine Chapel paintings. Rembrandt also drew his inspiration from the Bible for his painting *David and Saul*, the Samson series, and *The Jewish Bride.* These are only a few of the major works of non-Jewish Renaissance artists who depicted the characters and stories of the Hebrew Bible and Jewish life in Europe

As participants in the cultures of the countries in which they live, Jewish artists, like other artists, work in the traditions of their native lands or establish new artistic styles and schools of thought. Amadeo Modigliani, although famous for *The Jewess* (1909) and his portrait, *Jacques and Berthe Lipchitz*, of the Jewish sculptor and his wife, generally did not focus on Jewish subjects, and only sporadically used Jewish symbols in his works. Camille Pissarro is remembered as the patriarch of impressionist artists and is famous for his simple portraits and captivating landscapes. Other Jewish artists, however, are renowned for their Jewish subjects. Jacob Kramer is most recalled for his 1919 *Day of Atonement*, which portrays the simple piety of Jews from Eastern Europe. Marc Chagall, though a prolific painter, may be best known for his stained-glass windows of the twelve tribes of Israel in the synagogue of the Hadassah Hospital, in Jerusalem; his tapestry triptych of Abraham, Moses, and David in the main hall of the Knesset (Israel's parliament); and his *White Crucifixion* (1938), a painting portraying Jesus wearing a *tallit* (prayer shawl) as a loin cloth and representing the timeless tale of the Jew as a martyr.

In the field of sculpture, Sir Jacob Epstein achieved international renown for his portrait busts, and in particular for his bronze bust of Albert Einstein (1933). Jacques Lipchitz, mentioned as the subject of one of Modigliani's paintings, created his *Mother and Child* in New York between 1941–1945, after planning it during the two years he spent fleeing the Nazis in Europe. It now stands in the garden of the Israel Museum in Jerusalem. Chaim Gross's *The Ten Commandments*, a set of bronze relief tablets produced in 1970–1971, hangs in the synagogue at the John F. Kennedy Airport in New York.

Philosophy and Theology

Jewish philosophy began at the rabbinic academy in Baghdad with Saadiah Gaon (882–942). His main work, *The Book of Beliefs and Opinions*, was an effort to show the reasonableness of Jewish teachings, such as the existence and spiritual nature of God, the creation of the world, and the freedom and responsibility of men. The Torah and its many commandments, he argues, are not arbitrary divine commands, but have God's wisdom as their basis. Even the command to worship on the Sabbath has a wise justification: unless there was a set time and way of worshipping God, a religious community would have an unpredictable foundation and could not survive.

The next period of Jewish philosophy took place in Muslim Spain. Solomon ibn Gabirol's (circa 1021–1058) poem *The Crown of Royalty* became part of Jewish religious ceremonies and is still recited on Yom Kippur. Judah Halevi (1085–1141) wrote *The Kuzari*, a work that stressed the incapacity of philosophers to arrive at wisdom, since they are deaf to the messages of prophecy and divine revelation.

The Jewish philosopher who made the strongest impact on both Jewish and non-Jewish thought in the Middle Ages was Moses Maimonides (1135–1204). While he wrote extensively on the Hebrew Law, Maimonides also made important contributions to the fields of logic, law, medicine, mathematics, philosophy, and theology. His *Guide for the Perplexed* is a masterpiece of Jewish philosophical and theological literature, and was translated from Arabic to Hebrew and Latin in the early thirteenth century. In the seventeenth century, Baruch (or Benedict) Spinoza, a Dutch philosopher born in Amsterdam to a Portuguese-Jewish family, advanced such radical ideas about God, ethics, and nature, that he was expelled from his Jewish congregation. Though Spinoza founded no new school of philosophy, his influence on later philosophers was enormous. Especially important are his *Ethics* and his *Theologico-Political Treatise*.

The thoughts and writings of both Maimonides and Spinoza were in place long before the integration of the Jews into the mainstream of Western culture. After the emancipation of the Jews in Europe, when Judaism became more integrated into

other cultures, Jewish philosophers began to explore even further the world of thought outside Judaism. Moses Mendelssohn, who is credited with the development of Reform Judaism, paved the way. One characteristic of these modern thinkers was their ability to break old patterns of thought and create new ones. Among the most important Jewish figures in European thought was the French philosopher Henri Bergson. And in Germany, Karl Marx developed the ideas behind socialism and communism, and in Austria, Sigmund Freud developed psychoanalysis. Strong currents of modern Western thought derive in large part from the works of these individuals. A great many others who followed them, such as the twentieth-century philosophers Martin Buber and Hannah Arendt, have also made important contributions.

Education

Education, especially the education of the young, has always played a major role in Judaism. Traditionally, the main focus of Jewish education has been the Jewish religion. In the era of rabbinic Judaism, a network of *yeshivot* (centers for the study of the Law) developed with a focus on the Bible and Talmud. These academies educated a number of outstanding scholars. To a great extent, this type of education was not only the most respected form of learning for traditional Jews, but also the main form of learning until the eighteenth century.

The work of Moses Maimonides, as noted above, radically altered and elevated the status of the Jew in Western society. A more complete change in the Western viewpoint, however, evolved over a long period of time. In Europe, some Jews entered slowly into intellectual circles. Eventually some became respected political leaders, like Benjamin Disraeli; composers, like Jacques Offenbach; or scientists, like Albert Einstein and Niels Bohr. Gradually, Jews were admitted to prestigious academic positions in European universities. Then Jewish professors and scientists from continental Europe were able to obtain university positions in England and America when they fled Europe during the Holocaust.

As outstanding Jewish teachers and scholars in many fields gained prestige in American universities after World War II,

educational barriers for Jews in the United States began to crumble. The greatest change occurred with the elimination of the "quota system" at American universities. With the quota system, only a limited number of Jews might be admitted to any college class. This excluded many qualified Jews from the best schools. Once this system was abolished, Jews began to enter these prestigious universities in large numbers. In the many universities of the New York area, in particular, thousands of Jewish students took advantage of educational opportunities and became influential in the fields of medicine, dentistry, and psychiatry, among others.

Education in American universities opened opportunities for Jews in non-Jewish circles. In the field of education, Jews were able to teach and do research in public and nonreligious private schools. They also continued to work in Jewish supported institutions, such as Yeshiva University (an institution of higher learning for Orthodox Jews) in New York City and Brandeis University, near Boston, (established as a nonreligious university in 1948).

Jews in Europe and the Near East had a long history of activity in business. Indeed, the routes taken by Jews in the Diaspora were related in part to the Jews' involvement in banking and trade. In America, Jews also developed businesses of many sorts. The educational opportunities available in American universities, however, enabled Jews to enter mainstream professional and commercial lives in medicine, law, business, and civic and professional organizations to which they had previously been denied access.

Science and Medicine

The contributions of many Jewish men and women have been vast and significant to the advancement of the fields of science and medicine. Among them, the German physiologist and pathologist Oskar Minkowski (1858–1931) did some pioneering studies on diabetes and discovered the suppression of a pancreatic substance, later identified as the hormone insulin, in people who suffered from the disease.

Perhaps the greatest scientist of modern times was the German-born physicist Albert Einstein (1879–1955). He is most

■ *Albert Einstein, the father of the theory of relativity, lecturing on physics.*

famous for his theory of relativity, which became the foundation for the development of atomic energy. In 1921, Einstein received the Nobel Prize in physics. He settled in the United States in 1933, when the Nazi government of Germany took away his property and his citizenship. He was a supporter of Zionism; and in 1952 he was offered the presidency of the state of Israel, but he declined because he believed that he was not well suited for the position.

In 1953, Jonas Salk (1914–1995), an American physician and medical researcher, developed a trial vaccine against poliomyelitis (commonly known as polio), a dreaded disease mostly affecting children. Among the first people to test the experimental vaccine

were Salk, his wife, and their three sons. The vaccine was found to be safe and effective, and in April of 1955 it was released for use in the United States. As a result of this work, Jonas Salk received many honors, including a presidential citation from Dwight D. Eisenhower and a Congressional Gold Medal. He refused to accept any cash awards, and returned to his work to improve the vaccine.

Another American research physician, Baruch S. Blumberg (b. 1925), discovered an antigen that provoked antibody response against hepatitis B. His discovery led to the development by other researchers of a successful vaccine against the disease. In 1976, he shared the Nobel Prize in physiology or medicine for his work on the origins and spread of infectious viral diseases.

The following year, the Nobel Prize in physiology or medicine was awarded to another Jewish American medical researcher. Rosalyn Yalow (b. 1921) had worked to unravel the mysteries of the endocrine system and developed a method of measuring minute quantities of substances in the blood. This

■ *Men tending cactus plants on an experimental farm in Israel run by the Ben Gurion University Desert Research Institute.*

method, called radioimmunoassay (RIA), had a wide range of applications in the fields of science and medicine, but was particularly helpful in identifying the deficiency of insulin in the blood of diabetics. Her discoveries lent a whole new dimension to diabetes research.

Many other Jewish scientists have devoted their professional lives to the advancement of medical knowledge. These include such notables as: August von Wasserman, who developed the test for syphilis; Paul Ehrlich, who discovered the first drug to fight syphilis; Bela Schick, who developed the diagnostic skin test for diphtheria; Alfred Hess, who discovered that vitamin C could cure scurvy; Casimir Funk, who was the first to use vitamin B in treating beriberi; and Albert Sabin, who developed an oral vaccination against polio.

Literature

As discussed in Chapters 2 and 4, the Hebrew Bible is one of the most influential texts of the western world because of its content and its modes of expression. The works of Jewish philosophers and intellectuals have also helped to shape modern thought. In the literary sphere as well, Jewish writers and poets have achieved greatness.

Many Jewish writers focus on Jewish life and experience. The Swedish poet Nelly Sachs, who escaped the Holocaust, earned the Nobel Prize in literature in 1966 for her volume of poetry *Flight and Metamorphosis*. Jewish American literature has also flourished throughout the twentieth century. Mary Antin's *The Promised Land* (1912) is regarded by many as the most popular immigrant autobiography ever written. Abraham Cahan chronicled the moral questions that were raised by Jewish immigrants' search for success in *The Rise of David Levinsky* (1907), and these same issues are the subject of plays by Clifford Odets and Elmer Rice. Henry Roth, in *Call It Sleep* (1934), also reflects on the immigrant experience, as does Bernard Malamud in his early works, *The Assistant* (1958) and *The Magic Barrel* (1958).

In the second half of the twentieth century, Jews in America started to move from cities to the suburbs in greater numbers. Author Philip Roth wrote with humor about this changing

Jewish world in such best-sellers as *Goodbye, Columbus* (1959) and *Portnoy's Complaint* (1969). In his novel *Marjorie Morningstar* (1955), Herman Wouk wrote the story of a determined young woman who longs to rise above the confines of her middle-class Jewish family. Poet and short-story writer Grace Paley writes with sensitivity and humor about Jewish and non-Jewish characters in such collections as *The Little Disturbances of Man* and *Enormous Changes at the Last Minute*.

Three Jewish writers who made their home in America have won the Nobel Prize in literature. Joseph Brodsky (1940–1996) was born in the Soviet Union and won the prize in 1987, fifteen years after he began living in exile in the United States. His poetry was often about non-Jewish subjects, but two notable exceptions are his long poem, "Isaac and Abraham," and "The Jewish Cemetery near Leningrad." Isaac Bashevis Singer (1904–1991), born in Poland, filled his stories with the Yiddish culture and folklore of Central Europe. Saul Bellow, born in Canada in 1915, focuses his novels on Chicago and life in twentieth-century America. His characters are often Jewish, but the religious dimensions of their lives are not what is most important. *The Adventures of Augie March* (1953) and *Henderson the Rain King* (1959) are of universal concern. In this respect, Bellow joins the large number of American writers of Jewish descent whose works belong to the mainstream of American culture: Norman Mailer, J.D. Salinger, Susan Sontag, E.L. Doctorow, Isaac Asimov, and Joseph Heller.

Movies and Theater

American Jews had a prominent role in the early days of the motion picture and entertainment industries. For example, the Hollywood studio of Metro-Goldwyn-Mayer (MGM) was founded in 1924 by two Jewish immigrants: Samuel Goldwyn and Louis B. Mayer. Many Jews also achieved fame as film directors, actors, and actresses. Steven Spielberg, Dustin Hoffman, Barbra Streisand, and Gene Wilder are just a few examples.

The American theater world also benefited from the talents of many Jewish playwrights. Lilliam Hellman, Elmer Rice, and Clifford Odets were the creators of very popular and well-

received plays in the 1930s. The team of Moss Hart and George S. Kaufman created a string of Broadway comedy hits in the 1930s, and Neil Simon did it single-handedly from the 1960s through the end of the century, including such enduring comedies as *The Odd Couple* and *Brighton Beach Memoirs*. Perhaps the most renowned of American playwrights is Arthur Miller, whose classic drama *Death of a Salesman* won the Pulitzer Prize in 1949. In 1964, Sheldon Harnick and Jerry Bock created a musical from the stories of Yiddish storyteller Sholom Aleichem, about Tevye, a poor Jewish milkman in turn-of-the-century Russia. The result was *Fiddler on the Roof*, one of the most popular shows in Broadway history, which ran for 3,242 performances.

Jewish talents greatly influenced the field of comedy. Frequently, Jewish comedians starred in the resorts of the Catskills (the so-called "Borscht Belt") and in the vaudeville houses of New York City. They became humorous critics of themselves, their fellow Jews, and American society as a whole. On radio and television, Jack Benny and Milton Berle were immensely popular during the first half of the twentieth century, as were the films of the Marx Brothers, which are now considered classics of American comedy. In the 1990s, Jerry Seinfeld became a popular comedian and television star. The legacy of Jewish humor has grown with Woody Allen, Gilda Radner, Billy Crystal, Joan Rivers, and Mel Brooks.

Some Jewish humor is strongly influenced by the Yiddish traditions of Eastern Europe. Leo Rosten, in *The Joys of Yiddish*, points out that many Yiddish words and phrases have entered the general American vocabulary through "show business." Words like *yenta* (a gossip), *chutzpa* (nerve or audacity), a *kibitzer* (one who makes frequent comments without being asked), or phrases like *oy vey* (an expression of woe), and the expression "alright already" are familiar to many Americans.

Music

The Bible has much to say about music, singing, and dancing in praise of the Lord. The book of Psalms, which consists of 150 chapters, is the Jewish hymnbook, and King David is considered to have composed many of them. Many modern composers,

A joyous **horah**, or circle dance, celebrating the wedding of a Jewish couple.

both Jewish and non-Jewish, have written their own music for the Psalms and for many other portions of the Hebrew Scriptures. Handel's *Messiah*, for example, is based on texts of the Hebrew prophets.

For centuries, synagogue music and religious folk music were passed down orally. These were not written down until recent times. During the nineteenth and twentieth centuries, various collections have been published, among which is Samuel Naumbourgh's three-volume work, *Zemirot Yisrael* (Religious Songs of Israel), published in 1847. The most extensive collection of traditional Jewish religious music is the ten-volume work called *The Thesaurus of Hebrew Oriental Melodies* (1914–1932).

Many classical composers of Jewish descent developed their artistic work within the spirit of their European cultural

environments. These include great artists such as Felix Mendelssohn, Giacomo Meyerbeer, Jacques Halevy, Jacques Offenbach, Anton Rubinstein, Karl Goldmark, Gustav Mahler, and Arnold Schoenberg. The same could be said for the contemporary American composer, Aaron Copland, known for his orchestral work, *Appalachian Spring*.

Ernest Bloch is one artist who might be classified as a composer of Jewish music, even though he did not wish directly to follow Jewish folk music in developing his works. Many of the themes in his works echo the music of a synagogue service so much that they might be considered specifically Jewish. More recent Jewish composers, such as Leonard Bernstein, Aron Rothmuller, and Erich Sternberg, have used melodies derived from the music of Israel (particularly from Palestinian folk songs and dances). All of these composers, no matter what their chief source of inspiration might be, have made a significant mark on contemporary music.

In presenting the notable musicians of Jewish descent, it would be impossible to omit the names of Jascha Heifetz, Fritz Kreisler, and Isaac Stern, three of the great violin virtuosi of the twentieth century. Nor would a list of the world's great pianists be complete if it did not include Arthur Rubinstein at the top. In addition, the number of Jewish artists in the world's symphony orchestras and opera houses is almost endless. Certainly, in a survey of orchestras in the United States, Jewish membership would be highly impressive.

Jewish talents have influenced the world of popular music as well. Oscar Hammerstein was an operatic impresario who built at least ten opera houses in New York City. His son, Oscar Hammerstein II, in collaboration with Richard Rodgers, wrote the songs for many famous Broadway shows. Leonard Bernstein's *West Side Story* is one of the best known Broadway productions. Other popular Jewish performers include Neil Diamond, Bette Midler, Herschel Bernardi, Barbra Streisand, Paul Simon, and Art Garfunkel.

CHAPTER **8**

Judaism Facing the Future

During public worship of the Sabbath afternoon Jews ask their Lord, "Is there like Your people any other tribe on earth?" Indeed, historically, the Jews have proven to be an exceptional people, rich both in heritage and in the close bonds of kinship that have joined them together. Throughout most of this history, the Jews have been bonded by their shared religious traditions. Modern times, however, show a wide variety of Jewish cultures and religious beliefs. Unity among the Jews of today remains, but not without its challenges.

Religious Conflicts and Attempts at Resolutions

Traditionally, Torah has united the Jews. They discovered the importance of this religious foundation when the Northern Kingdom of Israel was captive in Assyria. During those years, the Israelites gave up on Torah, dispersed, and lost their identity. It was not until the Babylonian Captivity that the Judahites, or the Southern Kingdom, rediscovered the cohesive, molding force of Torah. Their rededication to the Law kept them united through their captivity, and they returned to Jerusalem after the captivity to rebuild the Temple. After the Second Temple was

destroyed, Torah and Talmud united the people of the Diaspora and kept them together throughout all their ordeals in many nations. The Enlightenment ushered in an era of flourishing Judaic philosophy. Moral and rational, this philosophy brought dedication to universal human values such as justice and freedom. These values became the heritage that united the people of a new Judaic tradition. They even felt that their old traditional ways of living often embarrassed them and separated them from the non-Jews they lived with. A new Judaism, Reform Judaism, was emerging with a view of God that differed from the Yahweh of the Torah and Talmud traditions. The God of Reform Judaism fostered the pursuit of justice and liberty. With this new movement and perspective came a division between Orthodox and Reform Jews.

Much later, Conservative Judaism tried to bridge the gap between Orthodox and Reform Judaism. This further split the Jewish tradition. A deeper chasm developed within Judaism when Reconstructionism emerged. Reconstructionist Jews placed less emphasis on the religious aspects of Judaism, substituted ideals for a personal God, and stressed the ethnic basis of Jewish unity.

The division of Judaism into different denominations, or groups, has caused a great deal of tension among its followers. Orthodox Jews see the modern movements as a betrayal of traditional Judaism. At first the Reform, Conservative, and Reconstructionist movements rejected traditional forms of worship. Then, in more recent years, each has reclaimed many of the traditional practices. Their doing so reduced some of the tension that was on the surface. However, in many cases, the non-Orthodox movements have given traditional rituals new meanings. They have taken their religious practices into new directions that are unacceptable to Orthodox Jews. An example is seen in the *bat mitzvah* ceremony for young women, introduced· by Reform, Conservative, and Reconstructionist Jews. Another example is that Orthodox Jews do not recognize the ordination of women rabbis. Statistics might indicate a return to traditional ceremonies among non-Orthodox Jews. Yet their alterations in the meanings of rituals and their adaptation to

modern ideals, such as feminism, often cause deeper differences and more heated tension.

The Holocaust and Its Memory

During the Holocaust in Europe more than six million Jews were murdered. It was an event that touched many Jewish families and made an indelible impression on the conscience of the world. Until recently, most Jews had vivid, personal recollections of family members who had been victims of Nazi atrocities. For a new generation of Jews, though, it is distant and not immediately felt. Children learn the history of these horrors as an academic lesson, or through books, such as those written by Anne Frank or Elie Wiesel. Thus, it has become difficult to pass on the reality of this terrible event. Keeping this memory alive is a great challenge in today's world. Many believe, with the cry, "Never again," that it is a lesson they must keep alive for all the world.

For a time, the lessons of the Holocaust made such an impression on Western Europe, and the whole world, that anti-Semitism seemed to have been greatly reduced. Recent events in France, Belgium, Germany, and Greece, however, have revealed a resurgence of anti-Semitism—graveyards have been desecrated, synagogues have been burned, and Jews have been physically attacked. The lessons of the Holocaust appear to be fading.

Likewise, as Eastern Europe has become independent of the Soviet Union, there is a real fear by Jews and non-Jews alike that anti-Semitism might arise again in this region. The communist rule of the Soviets kept ethnic and racial tensions under control, but, with the elimination of central Soviet rule, many of the old tensions might resume. Many Jewish movements in America and Europe have attempted to address this possible rise of anti-Semitism. They have urged the central power of the Catholic Church, the Vatican, to redistribute the 1965 papal encyclical *Nostra Aetate* (*In our age*) that condemned anti-Semitism as unchristian. To combat bigotry, many tens of thousands of copies of this letter from the Pope have been distributed in Eastern European countries. Still, the challenge of anti-Semitism remains a very real one.

The State of Israel

The Zionist movement for an independent Jewish homeland existed before the Holocaust. Since then, the support of many nations emerged when Europeans and Americans saw that many Jews who had been released from Nazi concentration camps at the end of World War II had no place to settle. Among Jews themselves, there had been opposition to a Jewish state, especially among the Reform Jews, who perceived the Diaspora to be a normal condition of Judaism. They also believed that Jewish life among Gentiles, in nations other than Israel, would lead away from non-essential religious rituals and foster the more universal values they considered essential to Reform Judaism. However, this changed after the Holocaust, and Reform Jews, indeed almost all Jews, rallied around the new State of Israel. Jews generally have a great loyalty to the new Jewish state, even though many Orthodox Jews do not see any religious reason to migrate there. Many Orthodox Jews see the Jewish State gradually chipping away at Orthodox religious practice. In January, 2002, for example, Israel's High Court, contrary to the Orthodox position, declared that those converted under non-Orthodox auspices outside of Israel must be recognized legally as Jews. Despite such difficulties, many Jews realize that the creation of the State of Israel normalized Jewish existence. How could Jews consider themselves a people if they lacked an independent nation to which they could belong?

But in setting up this nation, new tensions developed. By claiming the land that is Israel, the Jews displaced many other peoples, especially the Arab Palestinians. Palestinians also believe that their homeland is located in the region of Israel. Arab-Israeli tensions materialized in Israel in the Yom Kippur War of October, 1973. They have repeated themselves in the suicide bombings that have taken place in Israel and the military efforts of the Israelis to stop the Palestinians whom they view as terrorists. Although the intensity of Arab-Israeli relations seesaws back and forth, Israel is always threatened by these tensions. Indeed, they seem to be growing. All hopeful talk of two separate states in the territories of the West Bank and Gaza, which had raised hopes of peaceful co-existence, has

Russian Jewish immigrants arrive in Israel looking for a new homeland.

diminished, even disappeared, in the hostile climate of 2002. The Israeli-Palestinian conflict seems to offer little hope for peace.

Aside from these military tensions, Israel has its own internal problems. Israel views itself as a modern state, a member of the Western world, and in many ways more like the countries of Europe than like those of the Middle East. Jews who fled Russia for a new home in Israel were fairly easily assimilated, since Russian Jews had the education and skills that proved useful in adjusting to a Israeli life. Today, however, many Jewish immigrants are arriving from countries where they received no training or education. Assimilation of such immigrants is proving much more difficult. This situation, in combination with the low birth rate among Israeli Jews and an increasing birth rate among non-Jews in Israel, may shift Israel toward a society that is less Western in nature and more like other nations of the Middle East.

Threats to Judaism in America

Although some prejudice against Jews still exists in the United States, Jews generally have been free to progress economically and socially. Various Jewish organizations have been formed to counter prejudices and bigotry. The Anti-Defamation League has combated prejudice on a wide front. Hillel Foundations have been set up at universities to provide Jewish centers for students on campuses. The American Jewish Committee (founded in 1906), the American Jewish Congress (1933), and the World Jewish Congress (1936) continue to serve the causes of Jewish defense, foster interfaith dialogue, and promote social justice.

On the one hand, as some Orthodox Jews might see it, an odd consequence of reduced prejudice is that many of the younger Jewish generation now regard religious differences and interfaith marriages to be of minor importance. As such marriages become more common, the fabric of Jewish life runs the risk of unraveling. The interfaith family melds into the larger culture surrounding it, and risks losing the Jewish tradition that is so dependent on the Jewish family and meaningful Jewish family observance.

We can see this ambiguity in movements such as *Dabru Emet* (Speak the Truth), for example. This effort to bring people from different religions together strives to promote understanding and to stress what all religions have in common. Still, some Jewish leaders oppose this movement. They see in it a danger to Jewish identity: While general community might be built, Jewish community could well suffer, they argue, from the lack of focus on the special character and traditions of the Jews themselves.

In another direction, prejudice against Jews has at times given rise to desires among Jews to behave according to the "acceptable" norms of the culture. By changing their identifiably Jewish behavior, Jews could escape the limitations imposed by that culture on those who are "different." Though it has been necessary for Jews to assimilate into the cultures of the nations in which they live, reduced prejudice might allow Jews to live more freely and perhaps practice more traditionally. However, this adjustment to acceptable American behavior also runs the risk of a possible loss of Jewish identity. Assimilation is a real challenge for Jews in America.

Epilogue

After many centuries, despite the challenges and threats to its very existence, Judaism remains a vibrant religion and culture. Today, although Jewish people face many new challenges, they have developed the resources and riches, both religious and cultural, that promise a continued future. Through the frustrations that were so characteristic of their past, through trials and enslavement, victory and liberation, the Jewish people have remained a strong people, united by religious faith, cultural communality, close kinship, and a common heritage.

■ Cities of the World with Large Jewish Populations	
New York	1,900,000
Los Angeles	585,000
Miami	535,000
Jerusalem	422,000
Paris	350,000
Tel Aviv-Jaffa	341,000
Philadelphia	315,000
Chicago	250,000
Haifa	226,000
Boston	225,000
London	200,000
Moscow	180,000
Toronto	175,000
Washington	165,000
Kiev	100,000
Montreal	100,000
St. Petersburg	80,000

GLOSSARY

Anti-Semitism—Feelings against Jews as a religious or ethnic group of people.

Ashkenazim—Jews living in Germany, France, England, and later in Poland, Russia, and other middle European countries. They developed in this region their identifying religious practices and customs, and also the Yiddish language spoken mostly by the uneducated.

Bar Mitzvah—Literally, "Son of the Commandment." The ceremony celebrated on a Jewish boy's thirteenth birthday that commemorates his passage from childhood to responsible adult membership in the Jewish community.

Bat Mitzvah—Literally, "Daughter of the Commandment." Has recently been instituted by non-Orthodox Judaism to celebrate the maturity of a young girl on her twelfth or thirteenth birthday.

B.C.E.—"Before the Common Era." Used to designate dates that precede the Christian era.

Cabala (also Cabbala or Kabalah)—Mystic Jewish thinking and writing.

C.E.—"The Common Era." Used to designate dates after the birth of Jesus.

Covenant—Agreement, promise.

Diaspora—The dispersion or scattering of the Jewish people away from Israel.

Dietary laws—The rules governing food permitted and forbidden to Jews by the Torah.

Emancipation—The elimination by modern political governments of certain civil limitations that had been placed on Jews. This required adjustments of Jewish life to the new culture of the Enlightenment.

Exile—The period of captivity in Babylon (circa 586–538 B.C.E.)

Exodus—The term used to refer to the departure of the Hebrews from Egypt around 1220 B.C.E. It is also the title of a book in the Hebrew Bible.

Hanukkah (Chanukah)—The Feast of Dedication, a midwinter holiday celebrating the victory over the ruler Antiochus by the Maccabees and the rededication of the Temple.

Hasidism—A mystical movement, especially the one founded by Rabbi Israel Ba'al Shem Tov in Poland (1699–1761).

Hillel Foundations—Jewish student organizations founded at universities, named after one of the great teachers of ancient rabbinic Judaism.

Holocaust—A fire sacrifice; a destruction, usually by fire. The name given to the mass killing of the Jews by the Nazis in World War II.

Kaddish—A call to praise God's name, with the congregation's

response, expressing the hope that God's kingdom will come. It is used in worship and also at funerals as evidence of Jewish trust in God.

Kibbutz—A collective farm in Israel.

Kosher—"What is suitable or proper." Used to designate food and other items indicating that they are usable under Jewish law.

Maccabees—The Jewish family who led the revolt leading to independence in the war against tyrannical rule (167 B.C.E.).

Messiah—"Annointed." A deliverer who is expected to come.

Midrash—"Search for meaning." A commentary on the Scriptures.

Mishnah—The part of the Law that was passed down orally, then put into writing.

Mitzvah—"Commandment." Used to indicate God's commandments and the response to this divine call by fulfilling God's command.

Passover—Spring festival celebrating the time in Egypt when the Angel of Death passed over Hebrew homes.

Purim—A happy festival celebrating the time when Esther was queen of Persia and the Jewish people's lives were spared.

Rabbi—"Master" or "teacher." The term used for the spiritual leader and administrator of a synagogue.

Rosh Hashanah—The Jewish New Year and beginning of a ten-day period of repentance called the Days of Awe.

Sabbath—The seventh day of the week, dedicated to rest and worship.

Septuagint—The Greek translation of the Hebrew Bible, made in the third century B.C.E.

Synagogue—A building where the Jewish congregation meets for prayer, study, and assembly.

Talmud—The compendium of learning that is a basic source for Jewish law and codes.

Torah—"Law or instruction." Jews consider the Torah to be the divinely revealed instruction of the Scriptures.

Yahweh—The Hebrew name for God.

Yeshiva—Originally an academy of legal learning, now the term used for schools of religious education.

Yiddish—A language closely related to German, but with influences from Hebrew and the languages of Eastern European countries, used by the Ashkenazic Jews.

Yom Kippur—Day of Atonement for fasting, meditation, and prayer; the holiest day on the Jewish calendar.

Zionism—A movement to obtain a Jewish state in Palestine.

FOR FURTHER READING

Applebaum, Morton M. *What Everyone Should Know About Judaism*. New York: Philosophical Library, 1959.

Ben-Tor, Amnon, ed. *Archaeology of Ancient Israel*. New Haven: Yale University Press, 1992.

Bernstein, Rabbi Philip. *What Jews Believe*. New York: Farrar Strauss and Young, 1957.

Bokser, Rabbi Ben Zion. *The Wisdom of the Talmud*. New York: Philosophical Library, 1957.

Bright, John. *A History of Israel*. Third Edition. Philadelphia: Westminster Press, 1981.

De Haas, Jacob. *The Encyclopedia of Jewish Knowledge*. New York: Behrman's Jewish Book House, 1938.

Dever, William. *What Did the Biblical Writers Know and When Did They Know It?* Grand Rapids/Cambridge, U.K.: William B. Eerdmans Publishing Company, 2001.

Donin, Rabbi Hayim Halevy. *To Be a Jew*. New York: Basic Books, Inc., 1972.

Fackenheim, Emil L. *What Is Judaism?* New York: Summit Books, 1987.

Harris, Stephen L. *Understanding the Bible*. Fourth edition. Mountain View, Calif.: Mayfield Publishing Company, 1997.

King, Philip J. and Stager, Lawrence E. *Life in Biblical Israel*. Louisville: Westminster John Knox Press, 2002.

Mazar, Amihai. *Archaeology of the Land of the Bible; 1,000–586 B.C.E.* New York: Doubleday, 1990.

Seltzer, Robert M. *Jewish People, Jewish Thought*. New York: Macmillan Pub. Co., Inc., 1980.

Whiston, William (Translator). *The Life and Works of Flavius Josephus*. New York: Holt, Rinehart, & Winston, (No date given.)

INDEX

Aaron 27
Abraham (Abram) 9–10, 12, 14, 20, 21, 22, 23, 42, 70, 73, 75, 76, 78, 79, 80, 86, 104, 106, 121
Alphabet, Hebrew 22, 109
American Jewish Committee 138
American Jewish Congress 138
Amos 10, 42, 75, 82–83
Anti-Defamation League 138
Anti-Semitism 15, 64, 66, 67, 94, 135
Antiochus (Epiphanes) IV 50
Arabs 14, 20, 61, 66, 68, 136
Aramaean 20, 30, 36
Ark of the Covenant 28
Ascetics 51, 58, 99
Asherah 38, 39
Ashkenazic Judaism 15, 58, 59, 61, 62, 89–90, 93, 107, 111

Ba'al 30, 38, 39
Babylon 14, 20, 41, 44, 48, 49, 53, 132
Bar Cochba Revolt 53
Bar (Bat) Mitzvah 8, 103,104–106, 108–109, 134
Berit Hahayyim 107
Bible, *Amos* 82–83; *Chronicles* 31, 36, 75; *Daniel* 51, 75, 83; *Deuteronomy* 20, 72, 75, 80–81; *Ecclesiastes* 75, 83; *Esther* 49, 75, 83; *Exodus* 9, 23, 25, 26, 75, 76, 78, 80, 81; *Ezekiel* 44–45, 75; *Ezra-Nehemiah* 75, 83; *Genesis* 8, 10, 20, 21, 73, 75, 78, 79, 104,106, 110; *Hebrew Bible* 10, 18, 20, 23, 31, 32, 34, 36, 40, 45, 48, 49, 53, 54, 70–85, 114, 119, 120–121, 127; *Hosea* 75, 77, 110; *Isaiah* 42, 75, 108; *Jeremiah* 75, 81, 82; *Job* 75,83; *Joshua* 26–27, 75, 81; *Judges* 30–31, 75; *Kings* 31, 36, 37–39, 75; *Lamentations* 75, 83; *Leviticus* 75, 80, 81, 99; New Testament 18, 119; *Numbers* 75, 78, 80; Old Testament 18, 20, 70; *Proverbs* 75, 83; *Psalms* 75, 83–84, 114, 129; *Ruth* 75; *Samuel* 31, 34, 75; *Second Isaiah* 44; *Song of Songs* 75
Buchenwald 65

Cabala 58
Canaan 8, 9, 14, 20, 21, 22, 23, 24, 26, 30, 31, 35, 41, 46, 86

Cantor 12, 59
Chosen People 9, 10, 29, 42, 43, 90
Christianity 6, 15, 52, 53, 60, 63, 80, 89, 116, 118, 119
Circumcision (*berit milah*) 50, 104–107
Commandments (*mitzvot*) 90, 104–115; Ten Commandments 10, 23–24, 25, 28, 29, 43, 75, 80, 109
Common Era 18
Confirmation 108, 109
Conquest 24, 26, 41
Covenant 9, 12, 22, 28, 29, 30, 38, 44, 72, 86, 90; of Abraham 9–10, 21, 32, 34, 42, 104, 106; of David 32, 34, 35, 37, 39, 42, 43; of Moses 10, 23–24, 25, 42, 75

Daniel 51, 75, 83
David 32–35, 37, 39, 43, 121
Day of Judgment 43, 118
Dead Sea Scrolls 52
Death and Mourning 113–115
Diaspora 14, 15, 16, 17, 35, 49, 52, 53, 91, 119, 120, 124, 134, 136

Eastern Europe 67, 98, 99, 135
Egypt 14, 15, 18, 21, 23, 27, 41, 46, 56, 73, 76, 77; Egyptian Literature 23
Einstein, Albert 121, 123, 125
Enlightenment 16, 60–61, 62, 63, 90, 134
Esau 27
Essenes 51–52
Exile 9, 14, 36, 39, 41, 42, 43, 44–45, 46, 48, 49, 53, 72, 77, 81
Exodus 23, 25, 26, 44, 46, 75, 76–77
Ezra 46

Frank, Anne 65, 135
Freud, Sigmund 123

Germany 59, 62, 63, 64, 66, 89, 90, 92, 120, 125
God 9, 21, 23, 24, 27, 28, 34, 35, 38, 40, 41, 42–43, 72, 76, 86, 110, 116, 118, 122. *see also* 'El *and* Yahweh

Habiru 8, 78
Haggadah 77
Haggai 48, 75

Hanukkah (Feast of Lights) 11, 50, 51
Hasidim 58, 99, 101
Hebrews 8, 10, 14, 20, 21, 22, 23, 76, 78
Hebrew Union College 92, 94
Hillel Foundations 138
Hitler 11, 65
Holidays 11
Holocaust 11, 16, 64, 66, 68, 90, 123, 127, 134, 135, 136. *see also* Yom Hashoah
Holy Land 20, 58
Hosea 43, 75, 77, 110
Huppah (canopy) 111, 112

Iran 57, 66
Iraq 68, 119
Isaac 21, 27, 78, 79, 80
Isaiah 10, 42, 43, 70, 75, 108
Islam 6, 55, 57, 70, 116, 118, 119
Israel, Northern Kingdom 8, 14, 36, 37, 72, 132; Southern Kingdom 8, 14, 36, 72, 132; State of Israel 9, 11, 12, 14, 16, 29, 68, 69, 125
Isserles, Moses 90

Jacob 20, 21, 26, 27, 42, 73
Jebusites 31, 35
Jehovah 8, 118
Jeremiah 10, 43, 49, 70, 75, 81, 82
Jerusalem 14, 18–19, 31, 33, 35, 36, 37, 40, 41, 43, 44, 48, 49, 50, 53, 88, 91, 92
Jesus 29, 52, 121
Jewish Calendar 11
Jewish Theological Seminary 95, 102
Jews 6, 8, 9, 14, 16, 49, 55, 94, 119
Joseph 21, 73
Joshua 24, 26–27, 54, 75, 81
Judah 8, 14, 36, 37, 38, 39, 40, 41, 42, 44, 46, 48, 49, 72, 132
Judaism, Basic Beliefs 9–14, 86–103, 116–118; Branches 10, 12, 13, 15, 16, 17, 86–103; Conservative 16, 101–102, 109, 115, 134; Orthodox 16, 64, 68, 95–99, 102, 111, 134, 136, 138; Reform 16, 64, 72, 90–95, 107, 108–109, 113, 123, 134, 136; Reconstructionist 102–103, 134; History 18–45, 46–69; Modern 16, 62, 83. *see also* Ashkenazic *and* Sefardic Judaism
Judaea 8, 50, 51, 52, 53
Judges 30–31

Kaddish 114, 115
Kaplan, Mordecai 82, 103
Karaites 57, 75
Kibbutzim 67, 68
King 29; Kings of Israel 32, 33, 34, 35, 37; of Judah 36
Kosher 12, 88, 98, 99; Kosher Foods 12–13, 98

Law (Torah) 10, 11, 14, 21, 23, 24, 37, 39, 42, 44, 45, 46, 48, 49, 51, 54, 74, 75–81, 86, 102, 132; Dietary Laws 12–13, 99, 119 (see also Kosher); Moral and Ethical Teachings 10, 12, 43, 93, 118; Religious Laws 14, 29, 45
Levi 26, 28

Maccabees 51
Maimonides, Moses 56, 57, 88–89, 122, 123
Manasseh 36, 39
Marriage 15, 110–113
Mendelssohn, Moses 63, 123
Messiah 12, 16, 43, 53, 54, 86, 89, 90, 91, 118
Middle East 55, 56, 57, 138
Midrash 54, 88, 108, 115
Mishnah 54, 56, 88
Monarchy 29, 31, 32, 34, 35, 36, 37, 41, 43, 44, 46, 48, 70, 81
Monotheism 6, 9, 42, 43, 82, 86, 116
Moses 10, 14, 23, 24, 25, 27, 28, 29, 32, 42, 51, 52, 54, 56, 70, 76, 78, 80, 81, 86, 89, 98, 118, 121
Muhammad 29, 55, 60
Muslims 55, 58, 60, 63, 70, 120

Nathan 35, 41
Nazis 11, 16, 65, 101, 121, 125, 135, 136
Near East 6, 18, 21, 27, 29, 31, 36, 49, 53, 88, 124
Nebuchadnezzar 41, 44
Nehemiah 46, 49
Noah 20
North Africa 55, 56, 57, 88
Nostra Aetate (In our age) 135

Observances. see also Holidays
Omri 37, 39
Oral Tradition 54, 70, 75

Passover. see also Pesach
Patriarchs 21–22, 26
Pentateuch 15, 75, 78
Pesach (Passover) 11, 12, 13, 28, 35, 72, 77, 98, 115
Pharisees 51
Philistines 30, 32, 36
Priests 10, 28, 51
Promised Land 43, 76, 78, 86, 91
Prophets 35, 36, 42–43
Prophets (Nebiyim) 74, 75, 81–83
Purim (Feast of Lots) 11, 12

Rabbi 9, 10, 12, 15, 46, 53–54, 84, 88, 92, 94, 95, 98, 99, 102, 111, 134
Rabbi Isaac Elchanan Theological Seminary 96
Rabbinic Judaism 53–54, 55, 88, 89, 123
Reconstructionism 102–103, 134
Red Sea 27, 35, 76
Rehoboam 36, 39
Remnant 42, 43
Rosh Hashanah (New Year) 11, 12, 95

Sabbath 12, 13, 50, 95, 99, 132
Sadducees 51
Samson 30, 121
Samuel 10, 31, 32, 34, 35, 41, 75, 81
Sanhedrin 51, 52–53
Saul 31, 32–33, 34, 35, 121
Seder Meal 13
Sefardic Judaism 15, 57–58, 60, 61, 62, 88–89, 90, 107
Semites 20; Semitic Languages 20
Shavuot (Feast of Weeks) 11, 28, 109, 115
Sheloshim 114–115
Sheva'berakhot (Wedding Blessings) 111
Shiv'ah 114–115
Sinai, Mount 10, 11, 20, 23, 28, 29, 34, 54, 76, 86
Solomon 35, 36, 41, 119
Spinoza, Baruch (Benedict) 60, 122
Sukkot (Feast of Tabernacles/Festival of Booths) 11, 12, 115
Synagogue 8, 12, 17, 57, 59, 61, 97, 106, 107, 108, 119, 120

Tabernacle 28

Talmud 15, 54, 55, 56, 58, 61, 84, 88, 94, 96, 99, 101, 108, 134
Tanak 74, 75
Tehillim (Psalms) 83–84
Temple 18–20, 40, 44, 72, 88, 90; First 35, 41, 113, 119; Second 14, 51, 48, 52, 53, 113, 132
Tisha B'Av 11
Torah 6–8, 10, 11, 15, 49, 54, 57, 72, 74, 86–88, 89, 90, 98, 99, 101, 108, 122, 132, 134; see also Hebrew Bible, Pentateuch, and Law
Tribes of Israel (Jacob) 23, 26, 70
Tsidduq ha-Din 114
Tu B'Shevat 11

Union of Orthodox Jewish Congregations 96
Union of Orthodox Rabbis 96
Uzziah 36

Western Wall of the Temple, 70–72
Wiesel, Elie 65, 135
Wilderness Experience 24, 26, 29, 32, 46, 75
Work (on Sabbath) 13, 99
World Jewish Congress 138
World War I 64, 66, 95; II 16, 48, 65, 66, 90, 94, 101, 124, 136
Writings (Ketubiyim) 74, 75, 83–85

Yahweh 8, 9, 10, 22, 26, 28, 29, 34, 37, 39, 42, 44, 56, 81, 82, 88, 98, 104, 110, 134; as King 29, 31, 34, 37; Yahwism 41, 43
Yarmulke 72, 94, 95
Yeshiva 55, 96, 123
Yeshiva University 96, 124
Yiddish 58, 60, 96, 128, 129
Yom HaAtzmaut 11
Yom Hashoah 11; see also Holocaust
Yom Kippur (Day of Atonement) 11, 12, 59, 88, 115, 122
Yom Kippur War 136

Zealots 52
Zechariah 48, 75
Zephaniah 43, 75
Zionism 67, 68, 91, 93, 94, 125, 136